Easy Coloring Book for Adults with Dementia

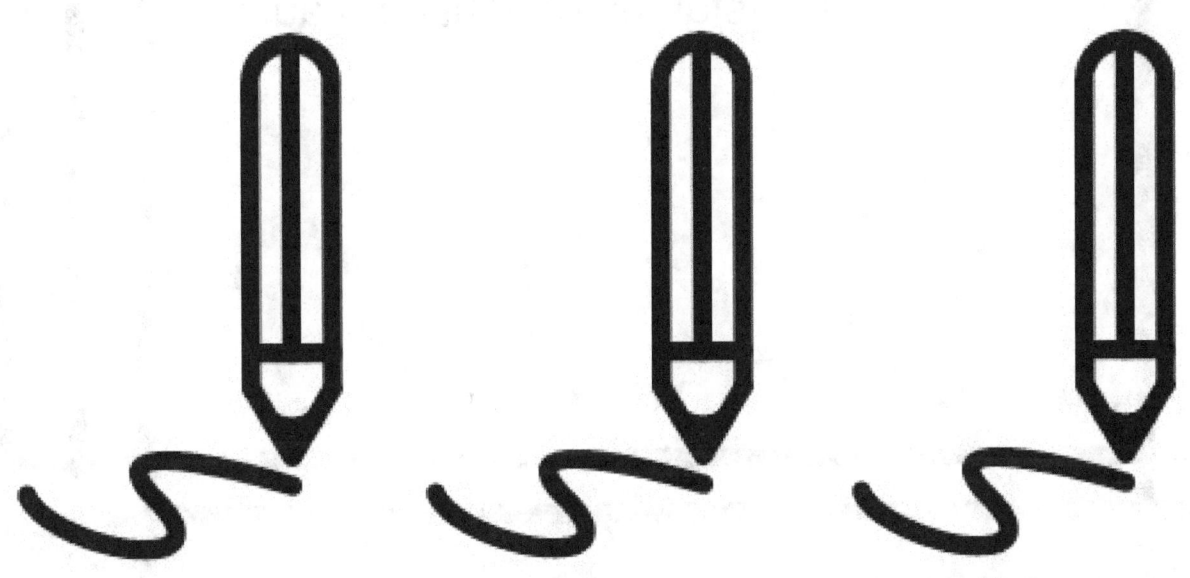

Hello!

Many thanks for your purchase and we hope that you enjoy this book.

You are most welcome to leave a review as it lets us know how we are doing and make any improvements where required.

For all inquiries, please send an email to info@starshinebright.com.au

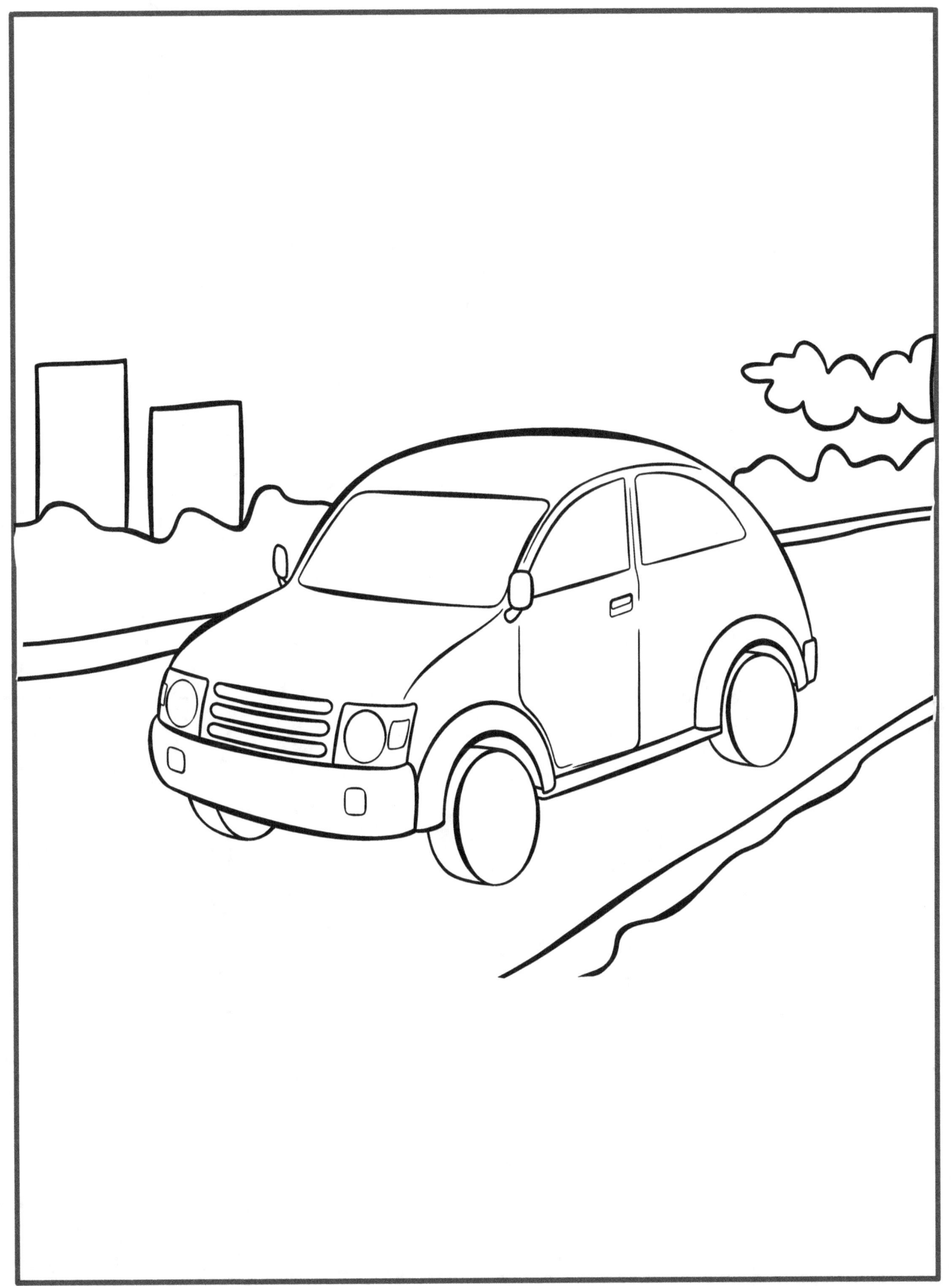

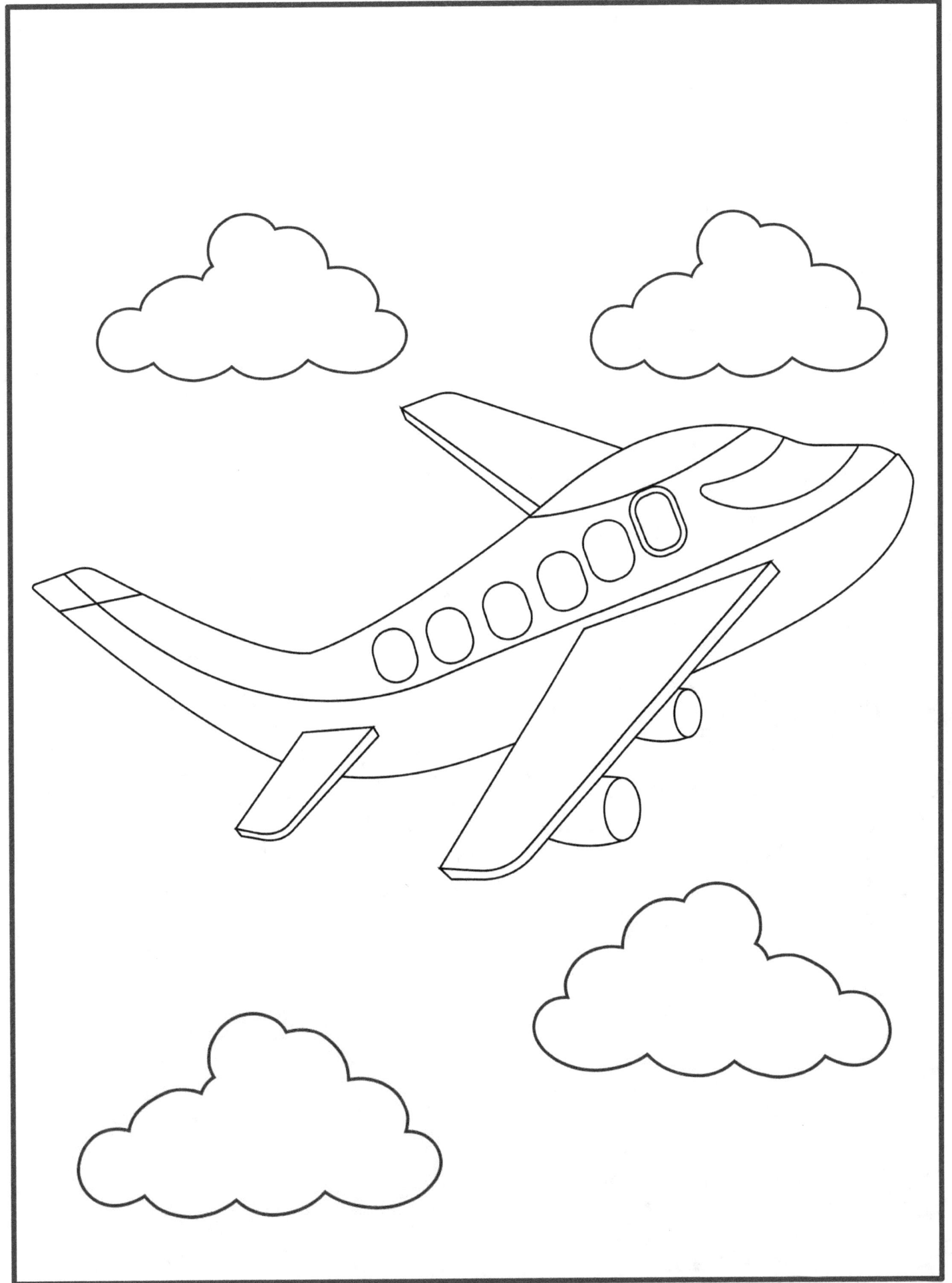

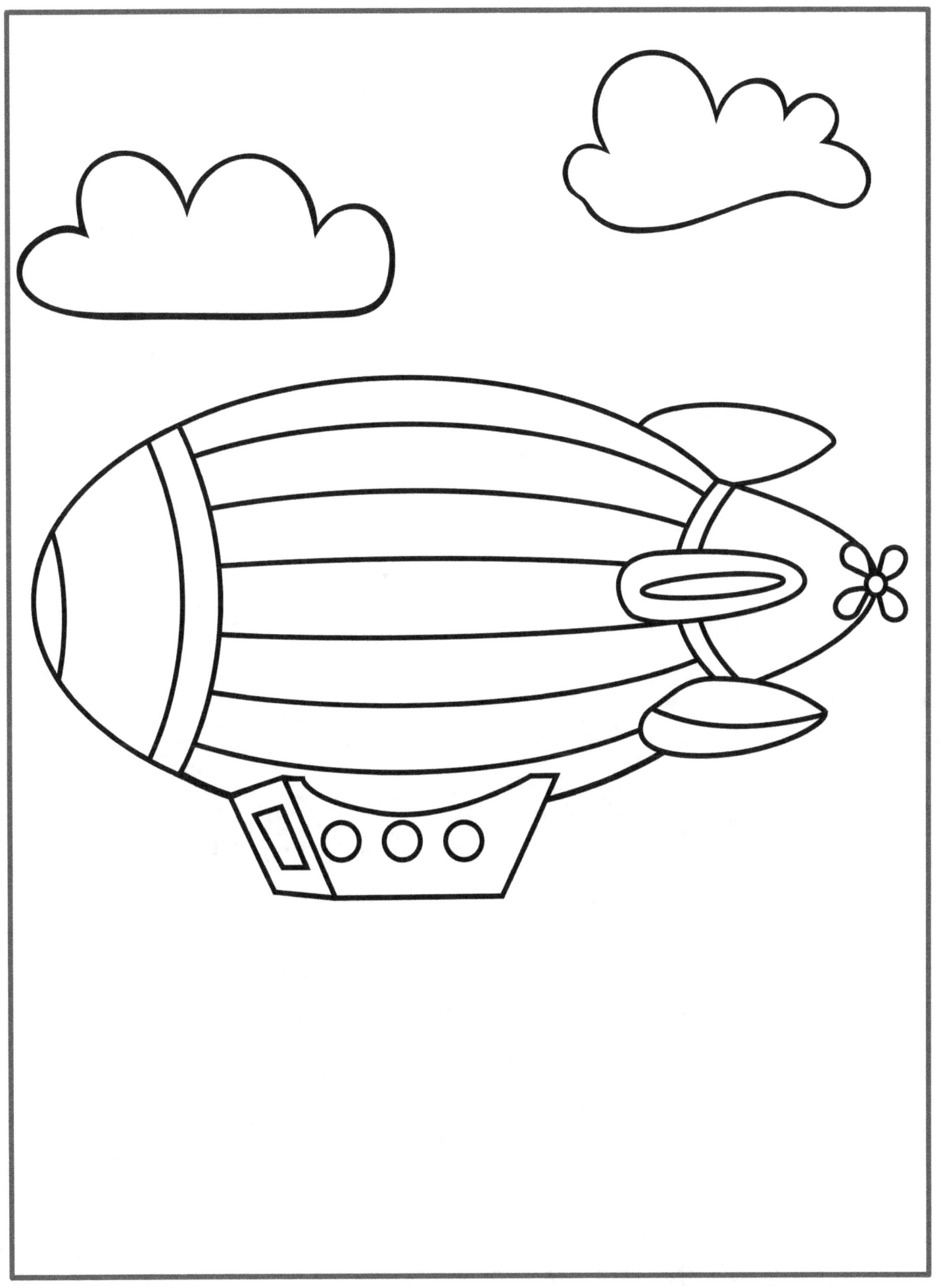

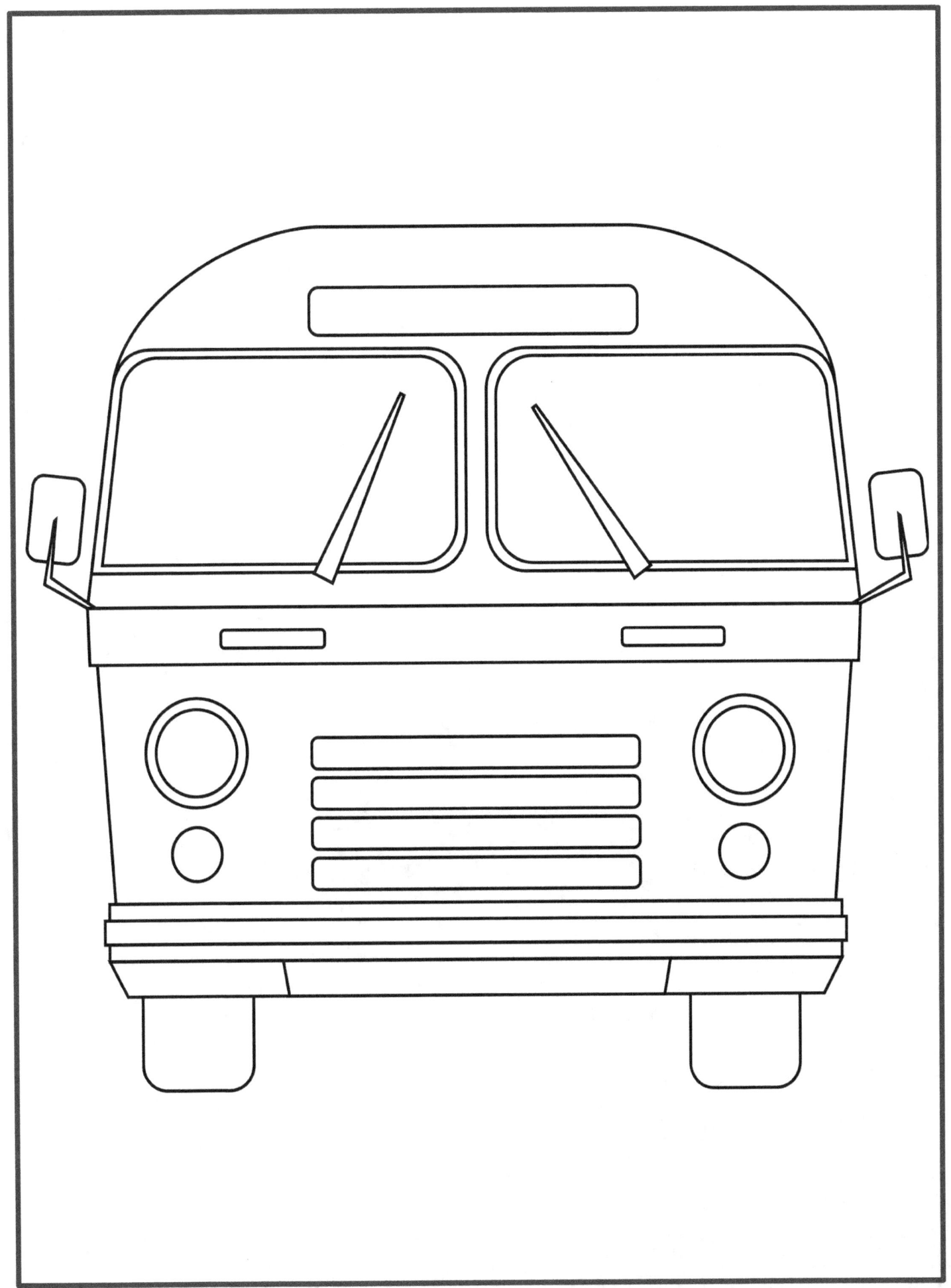

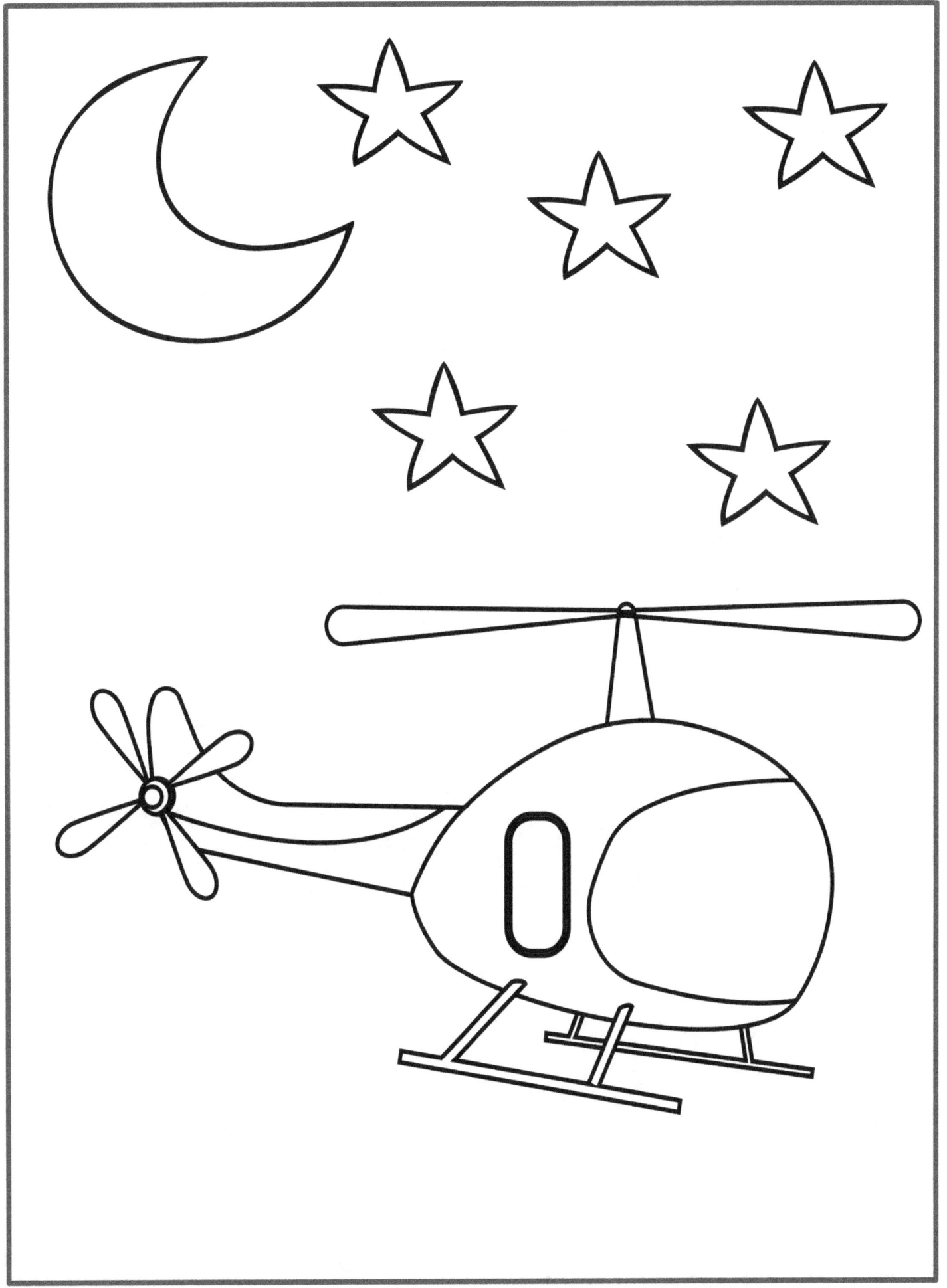

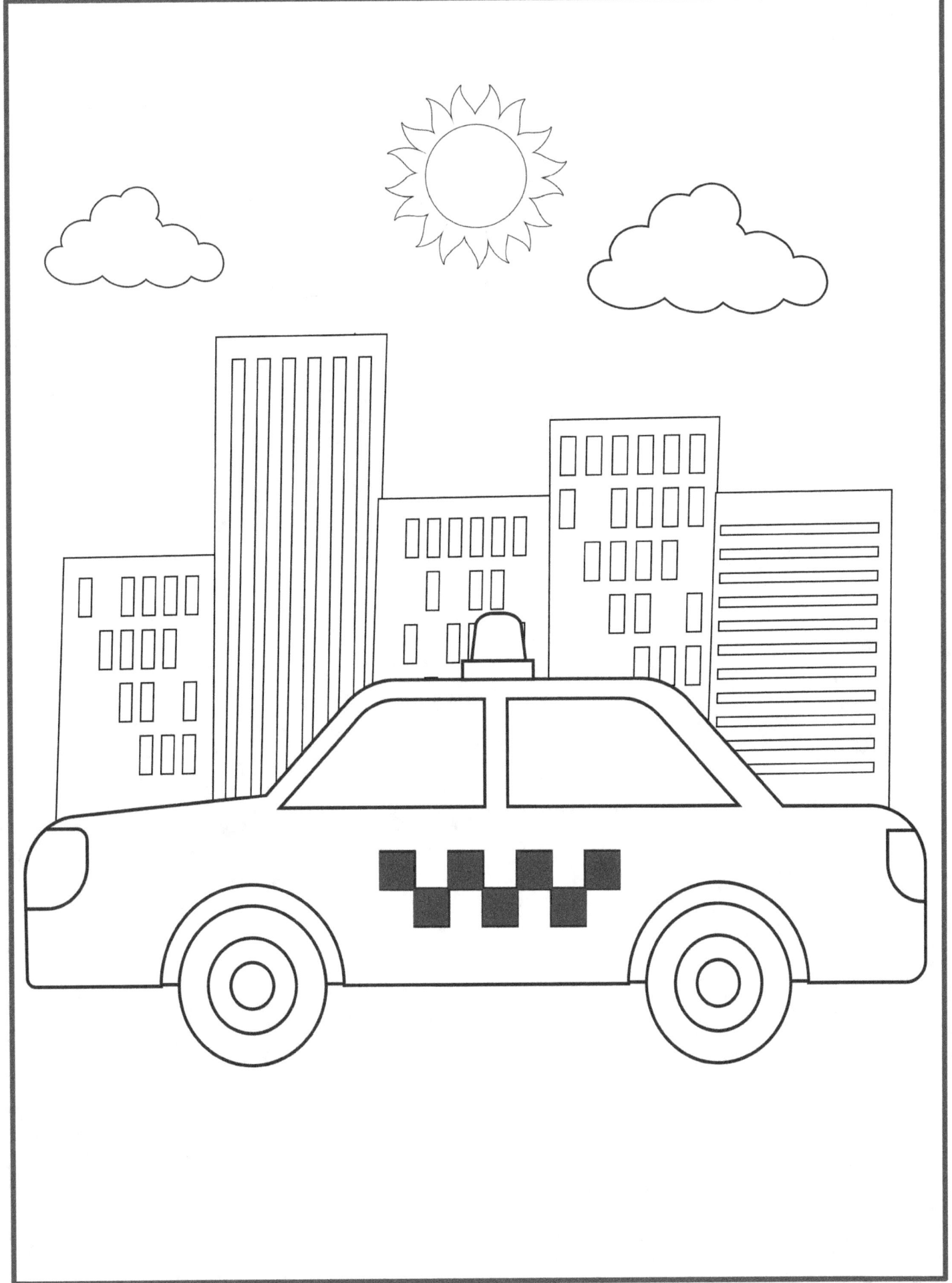

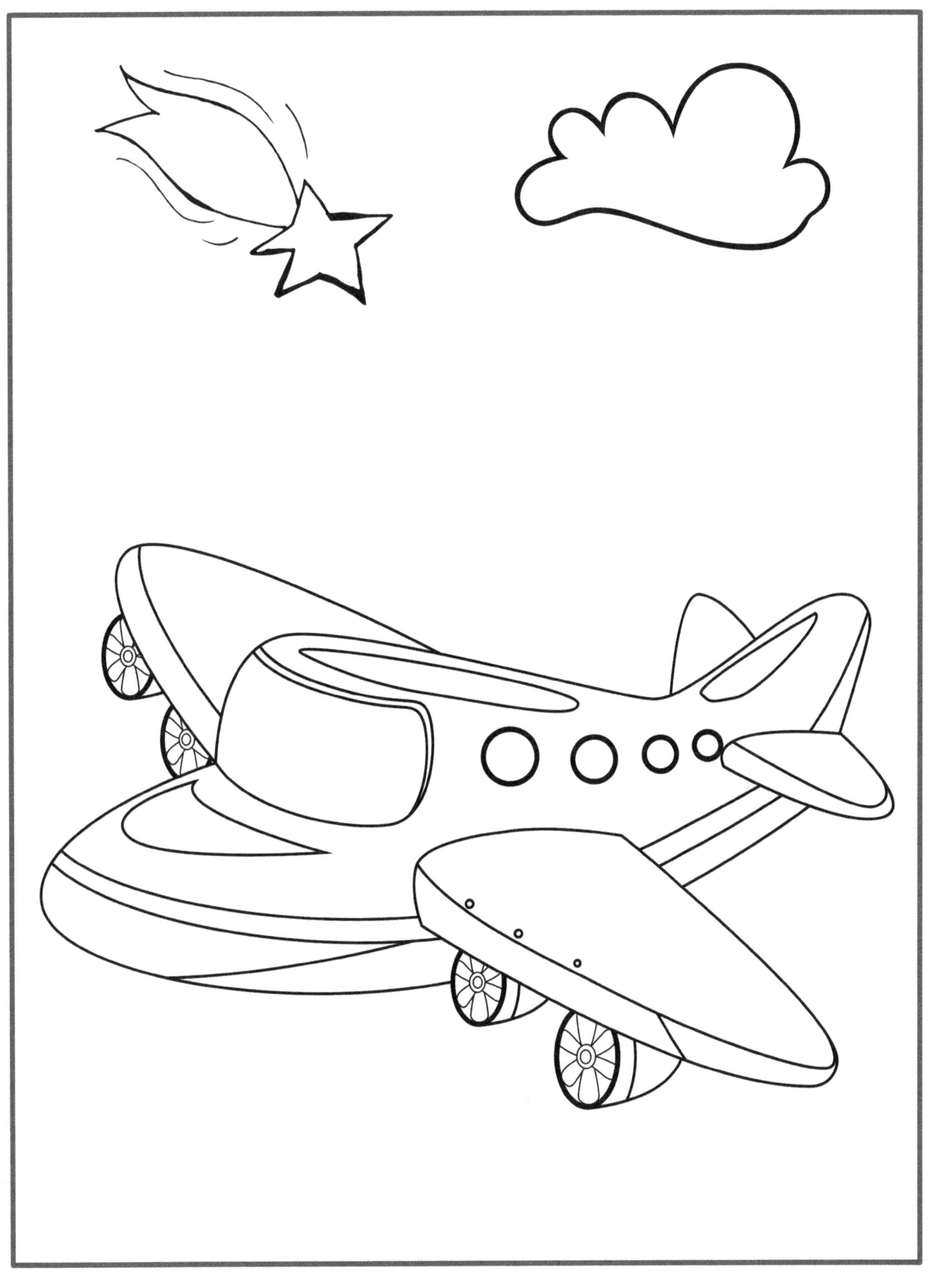

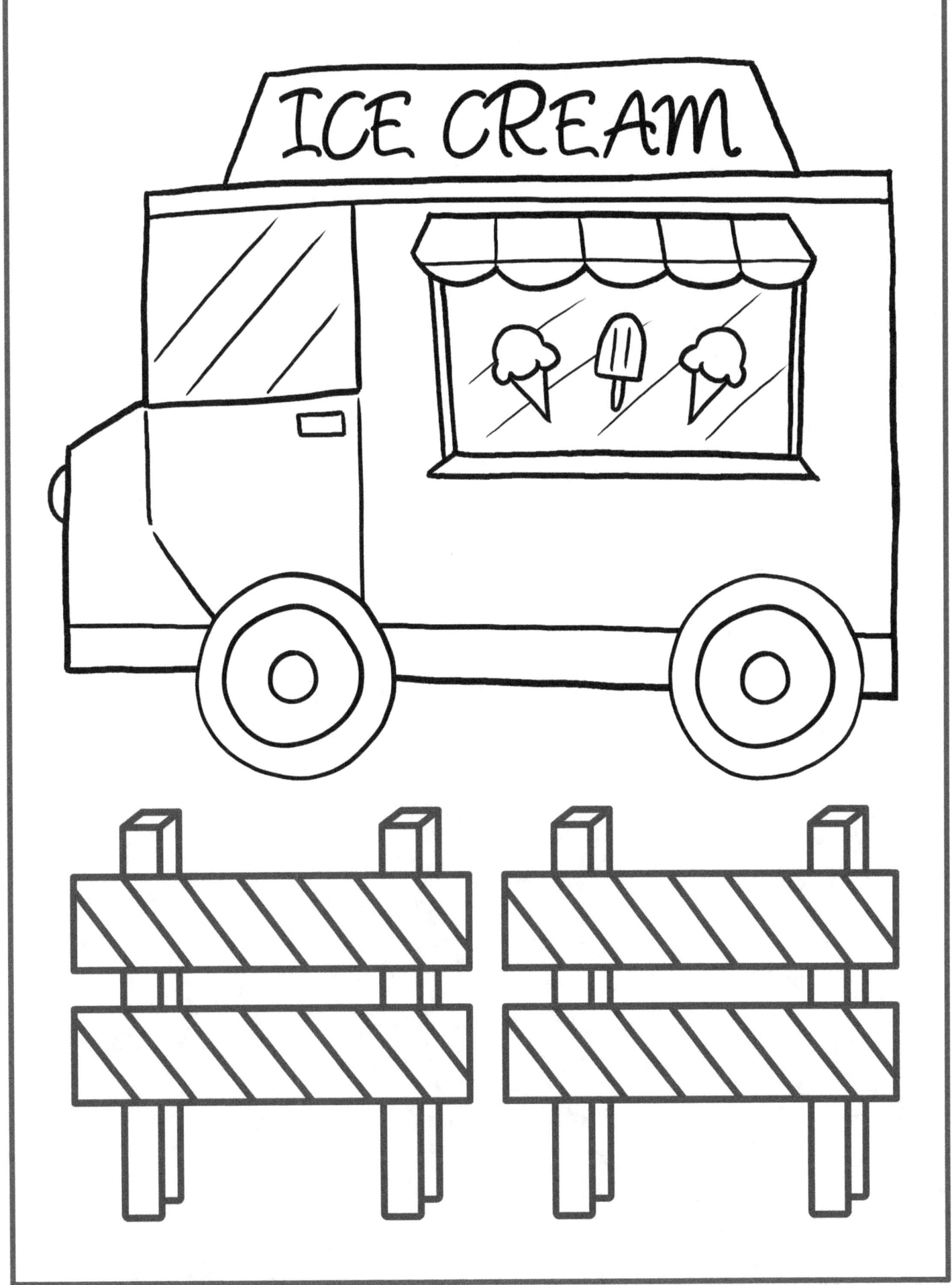

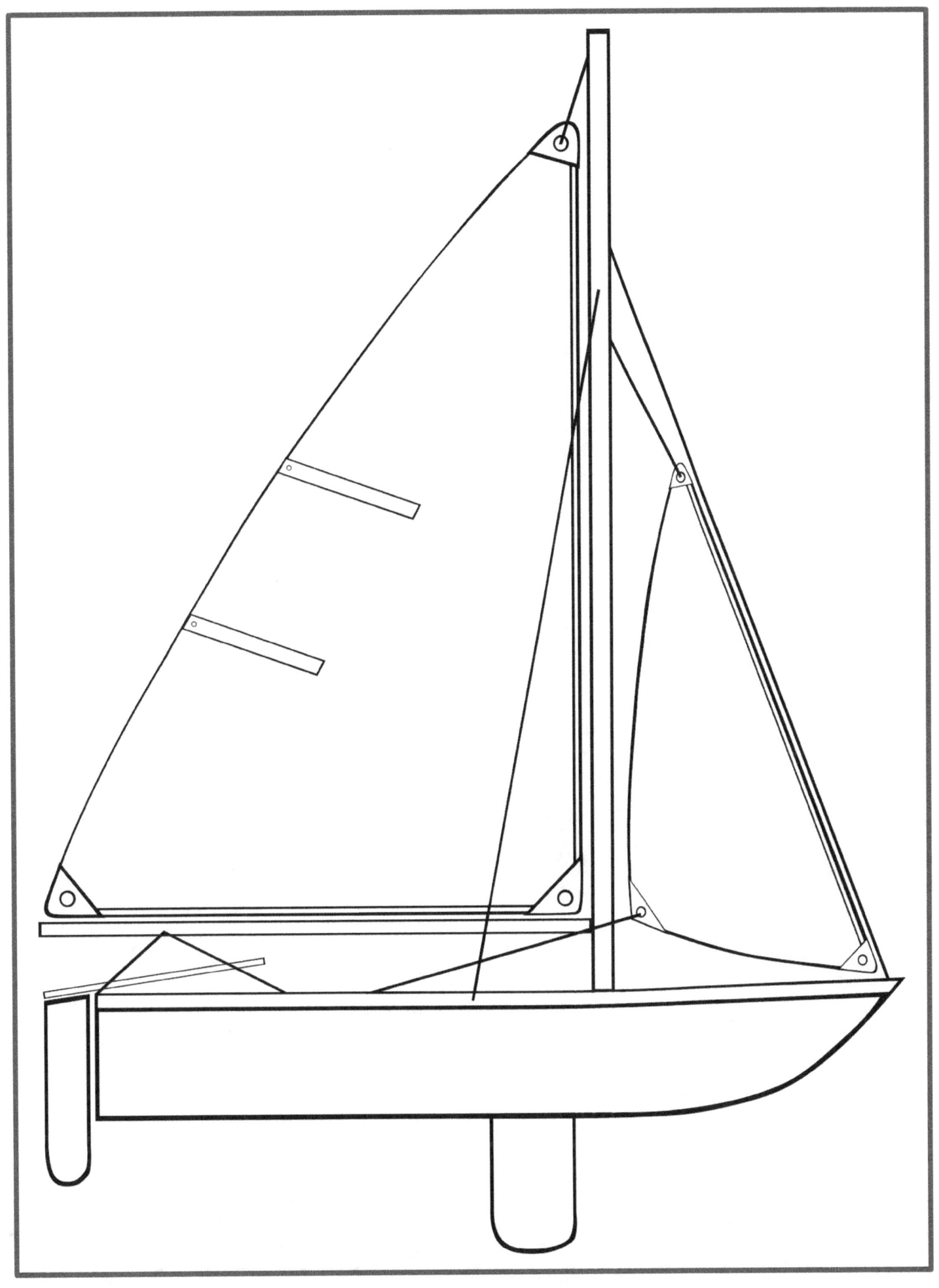

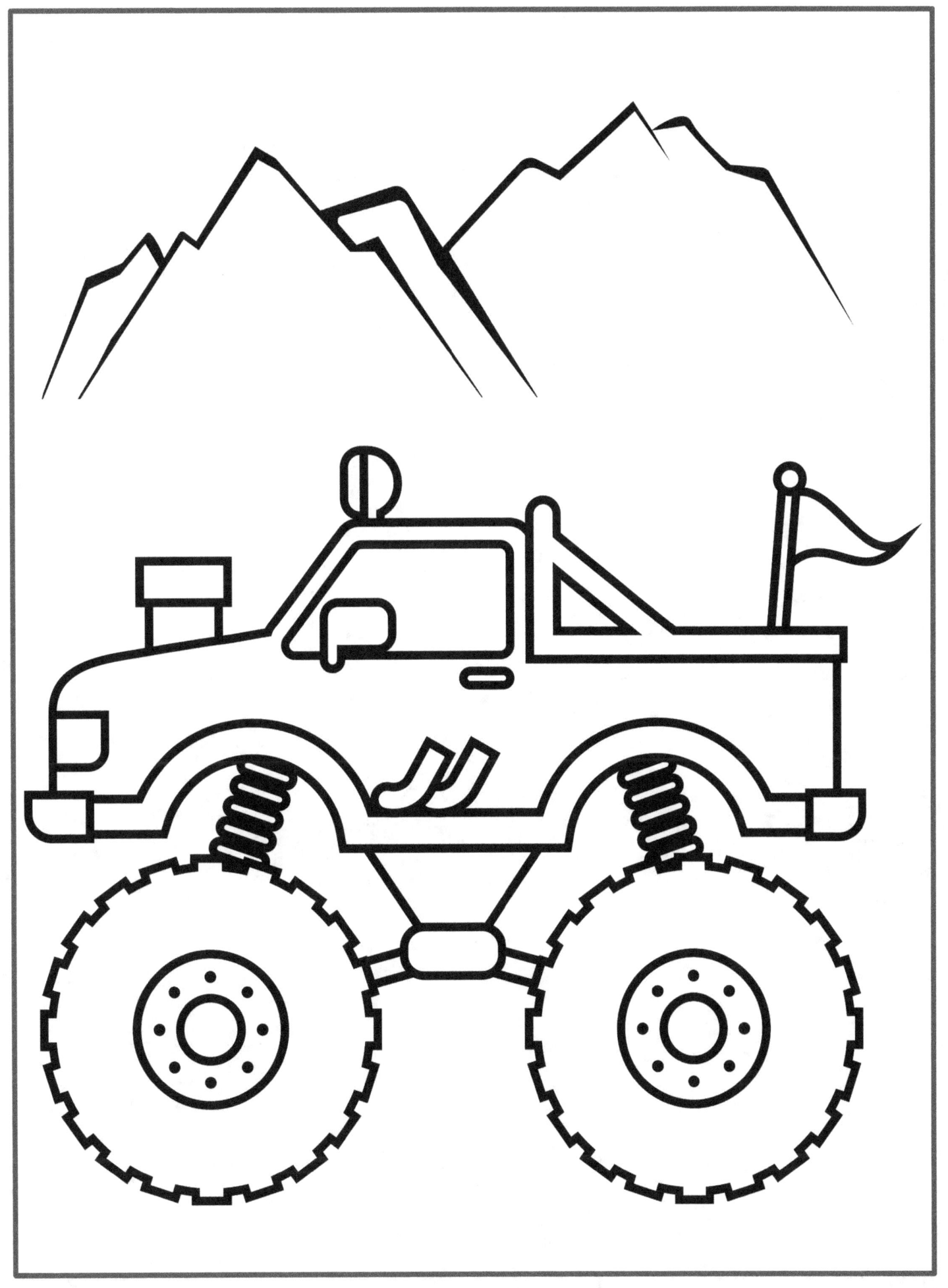

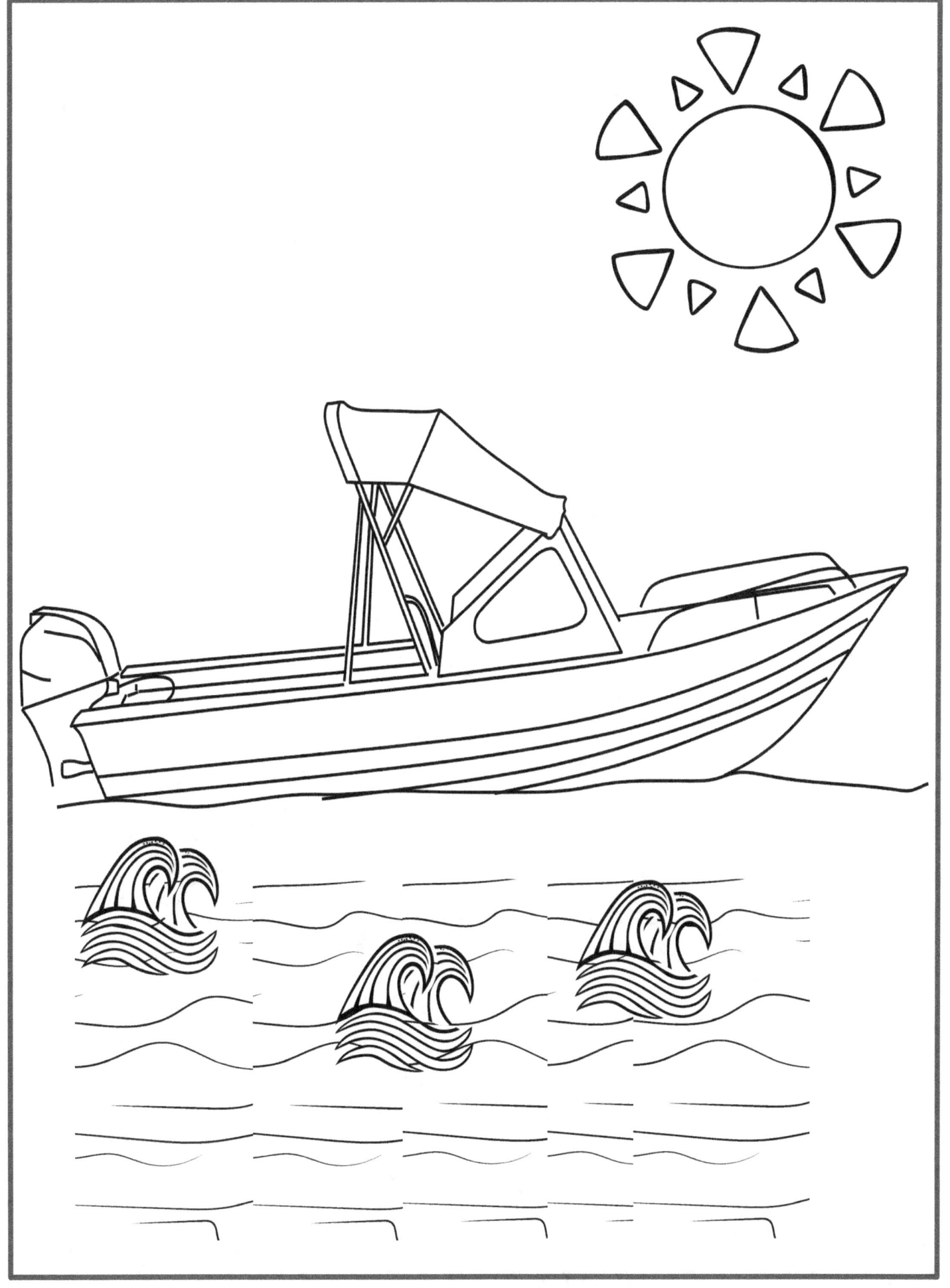

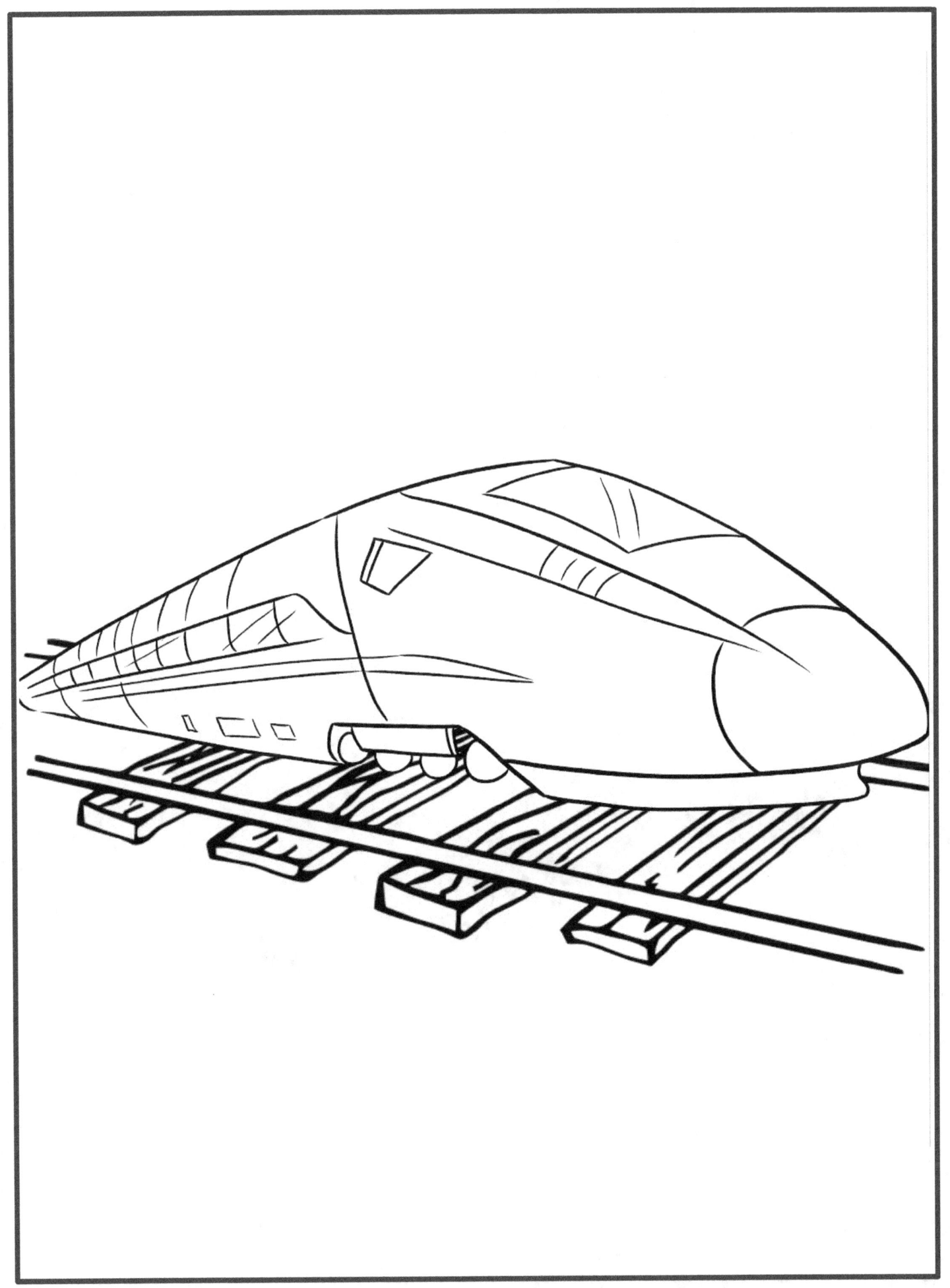

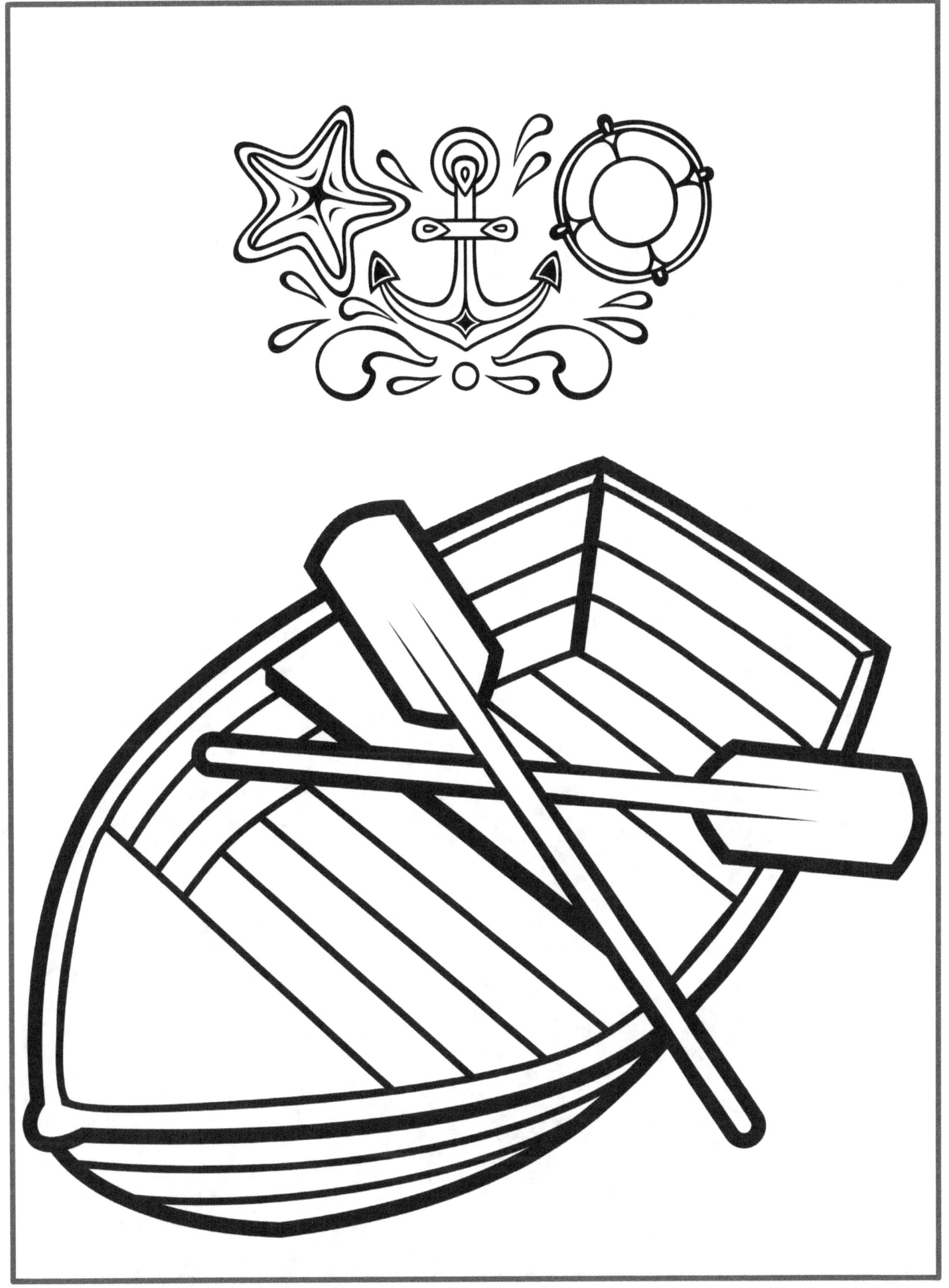

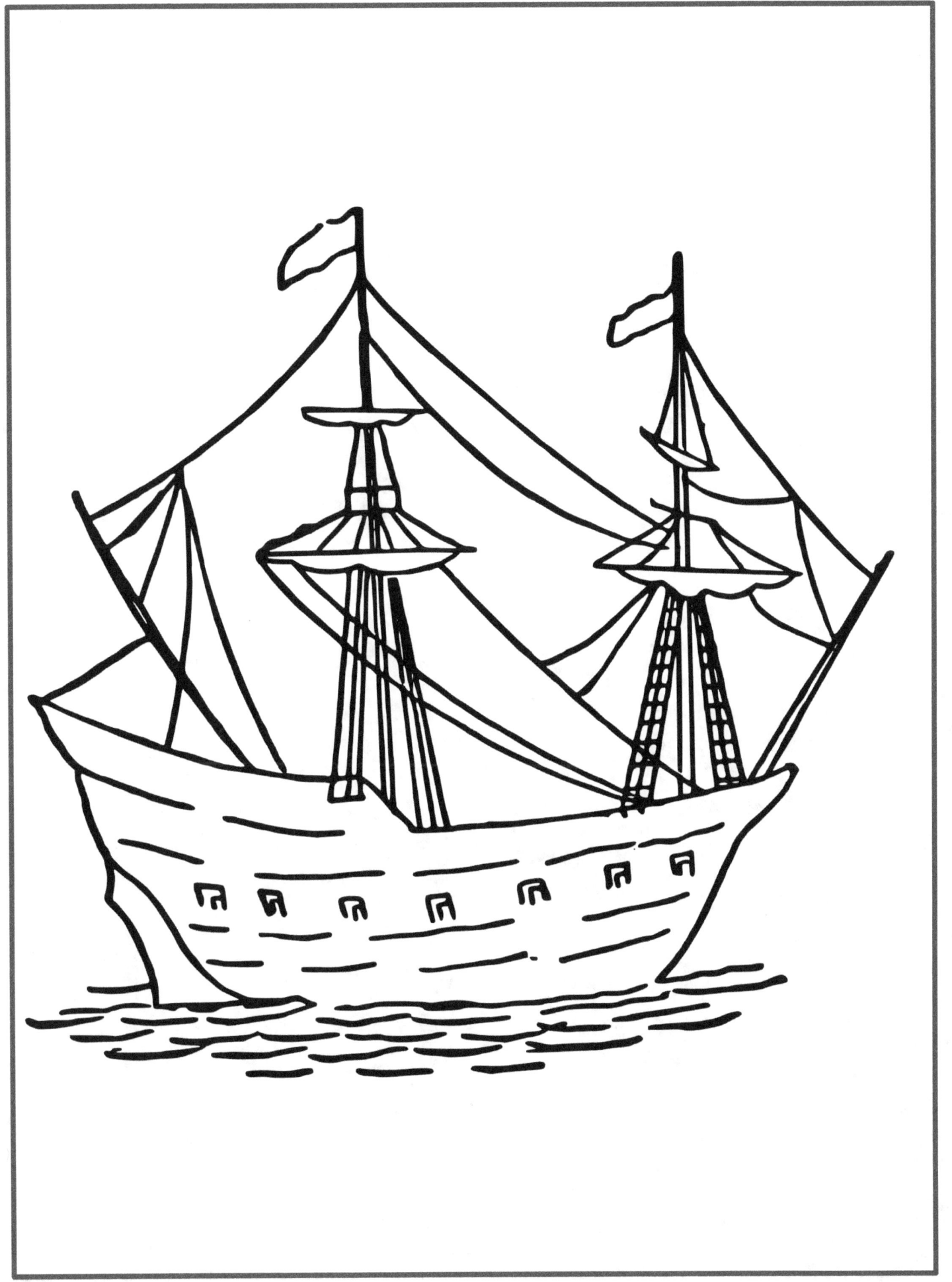

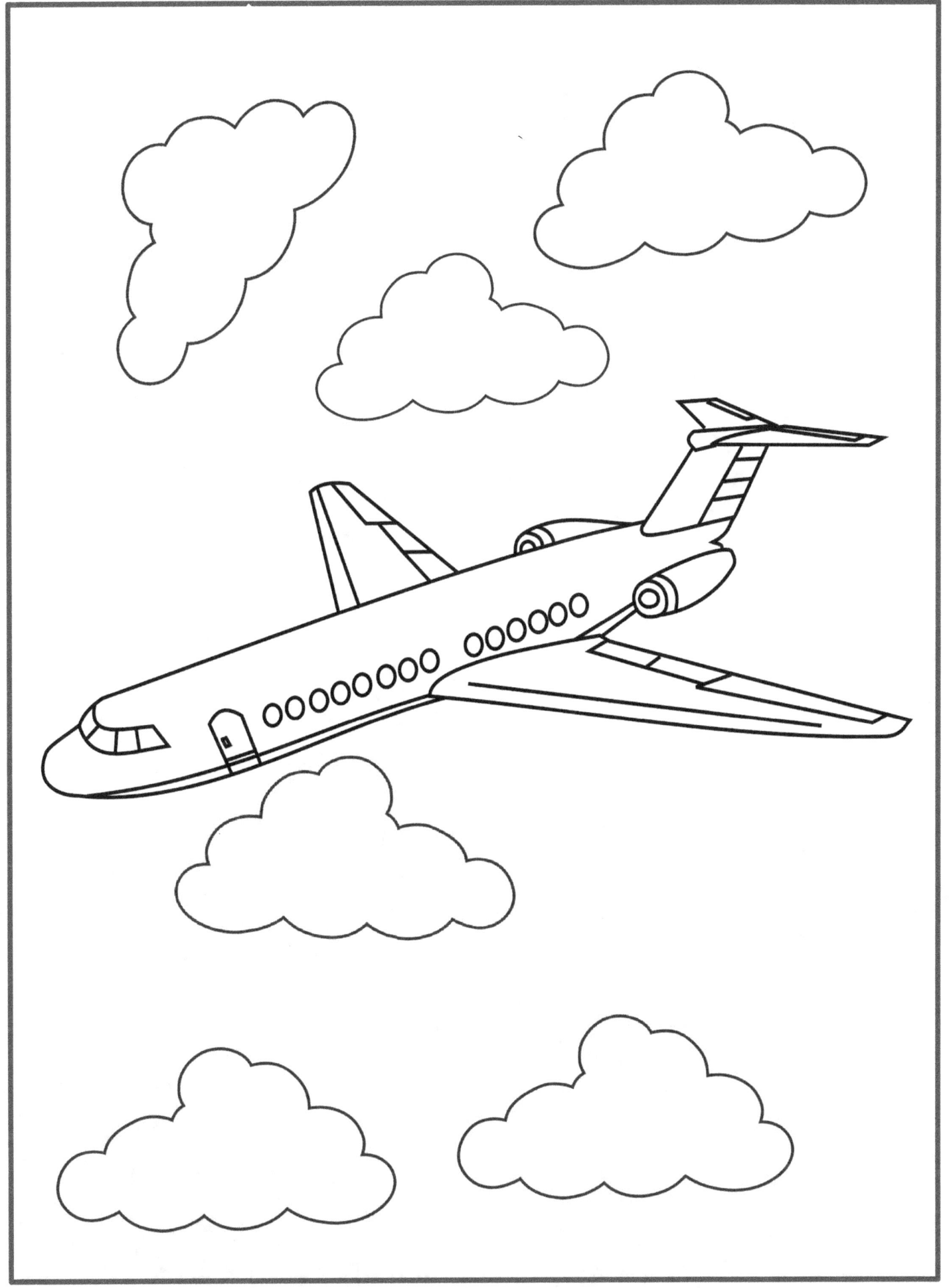

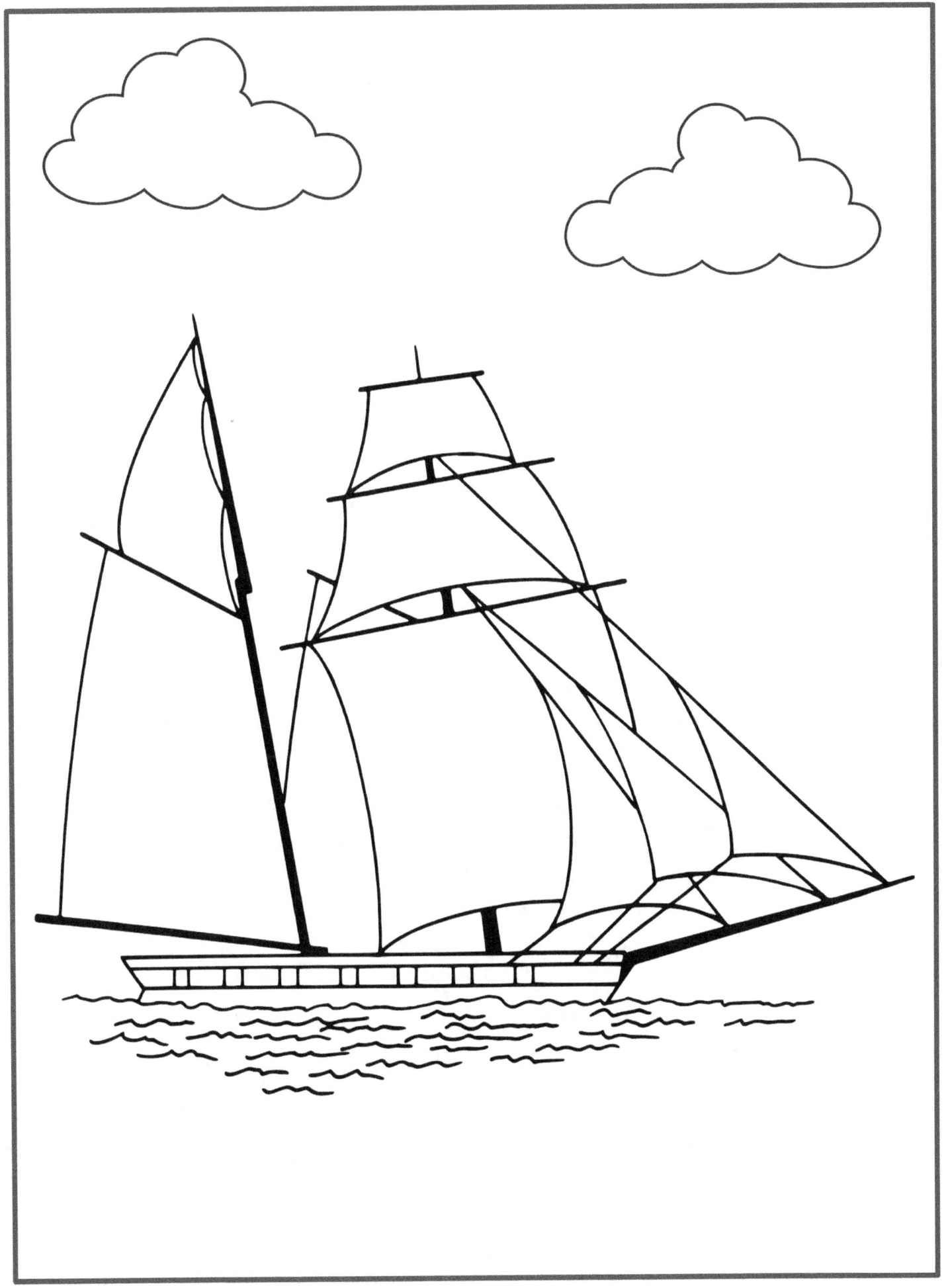

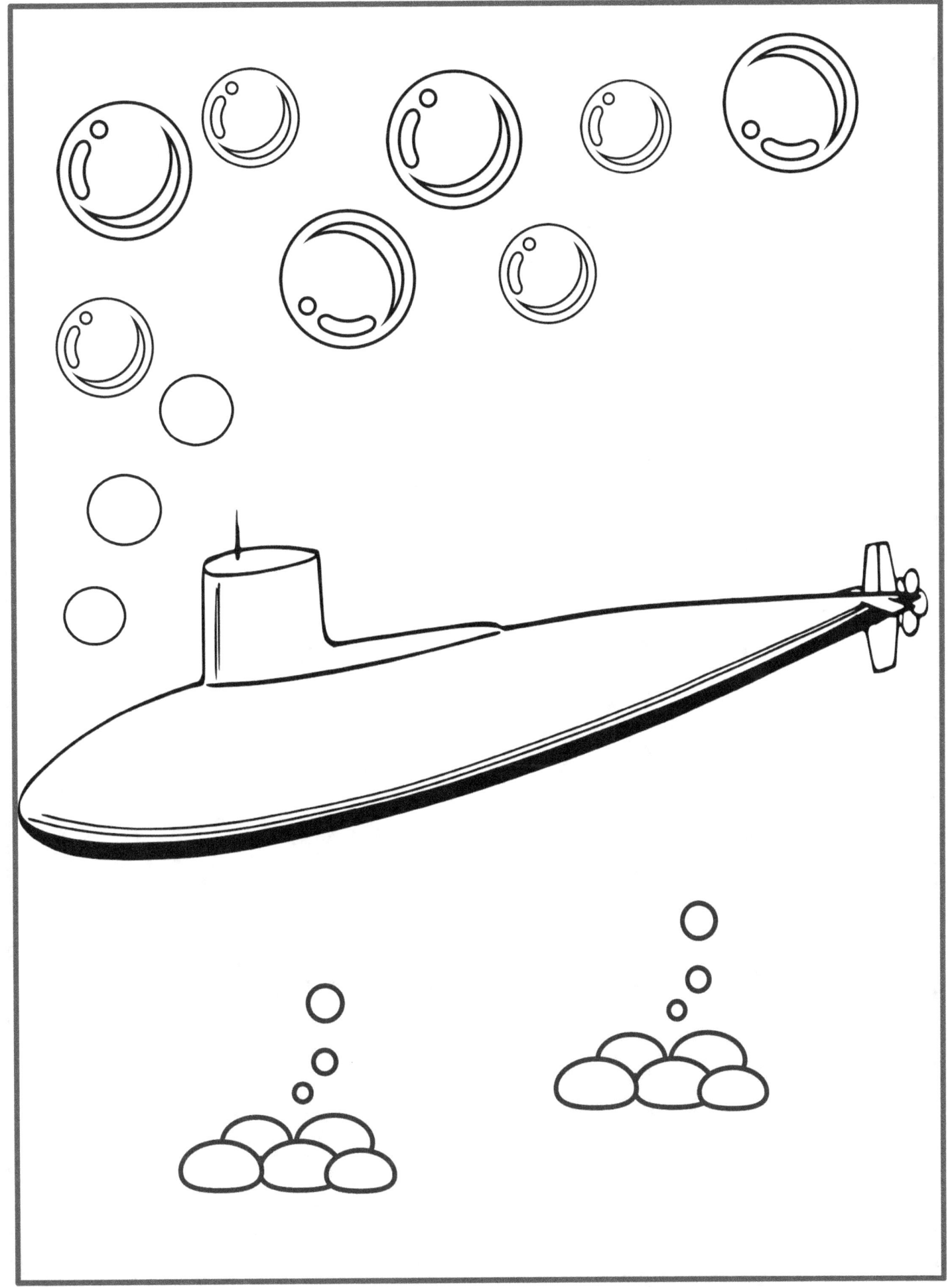

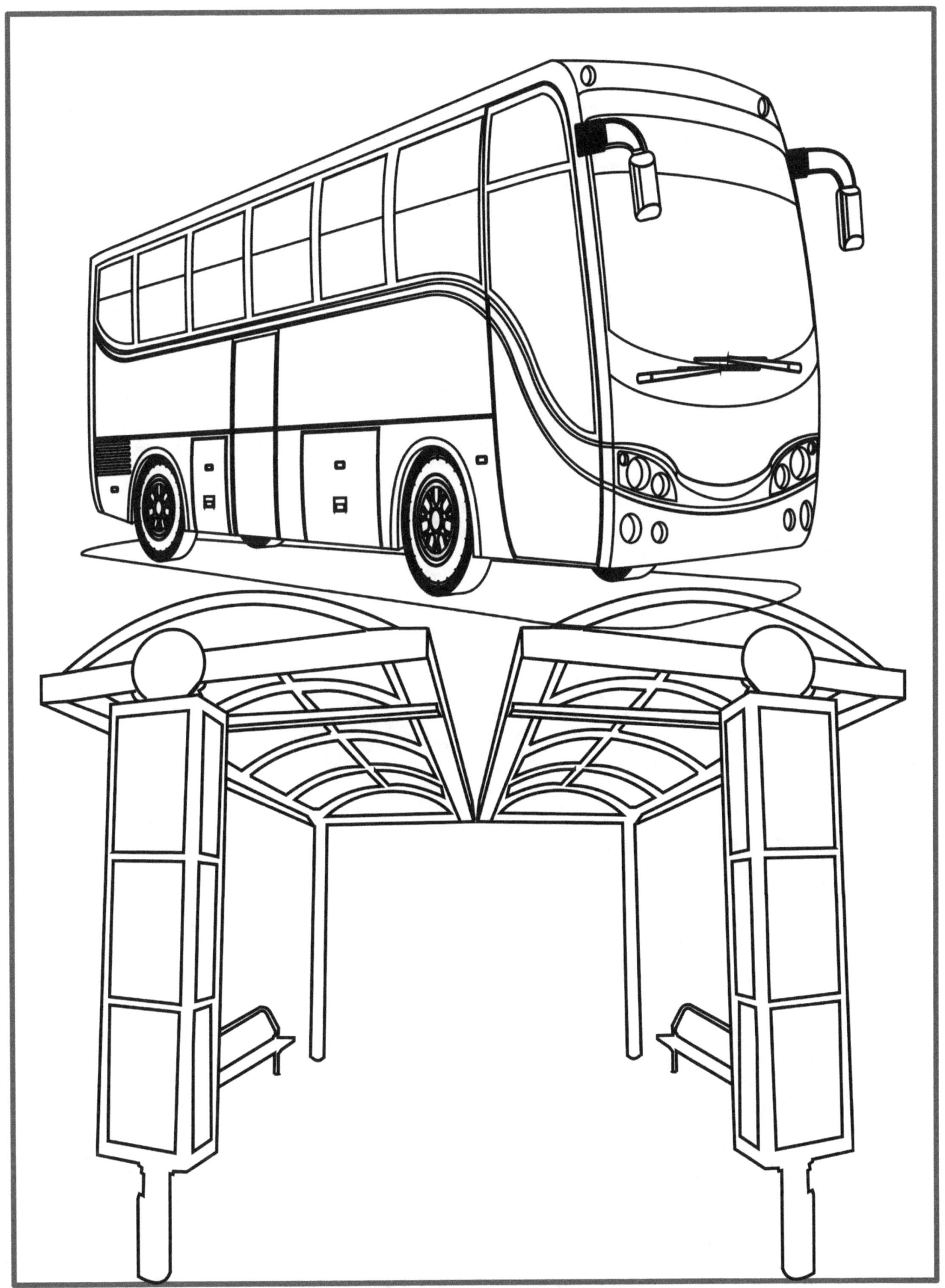

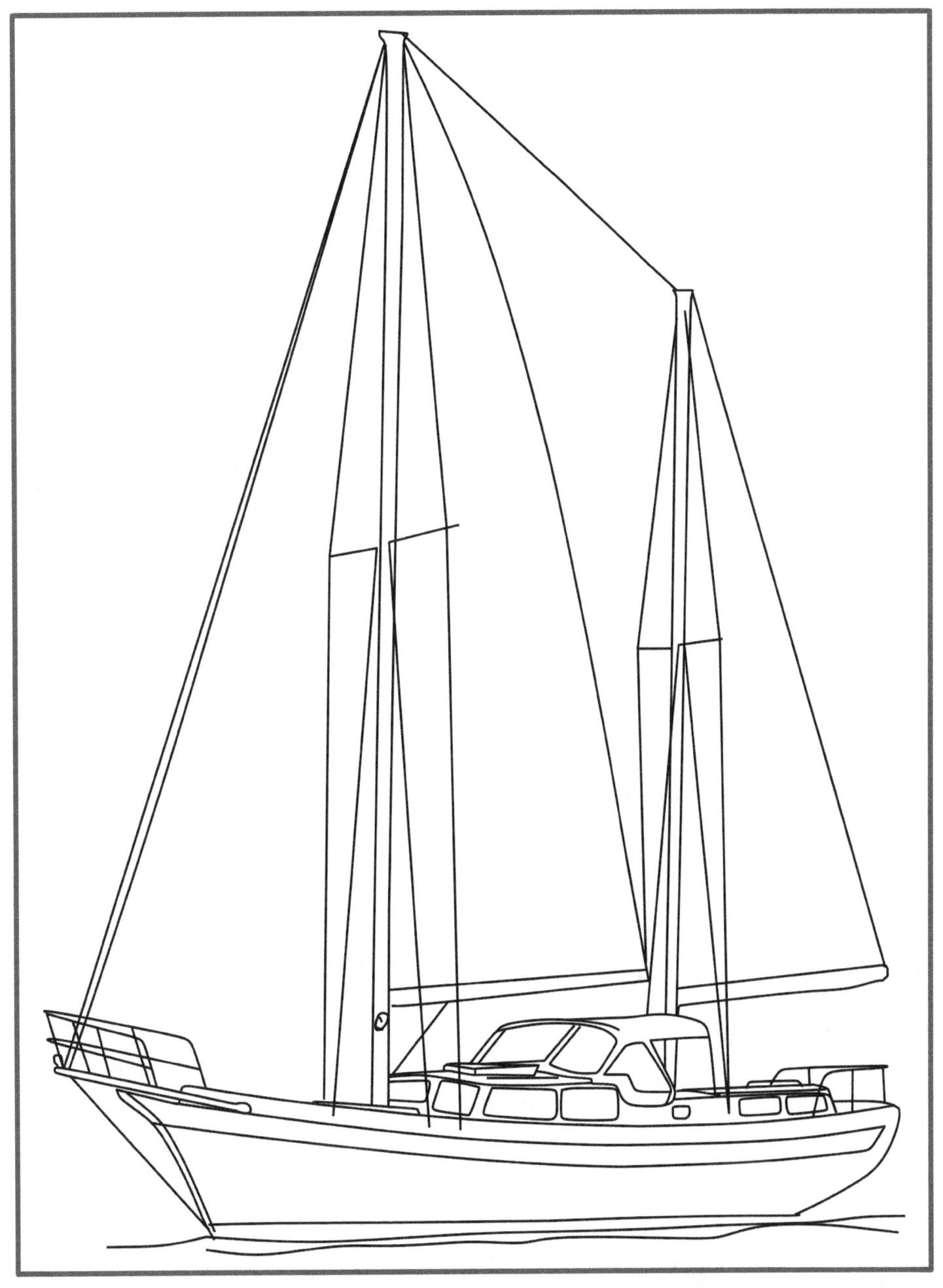

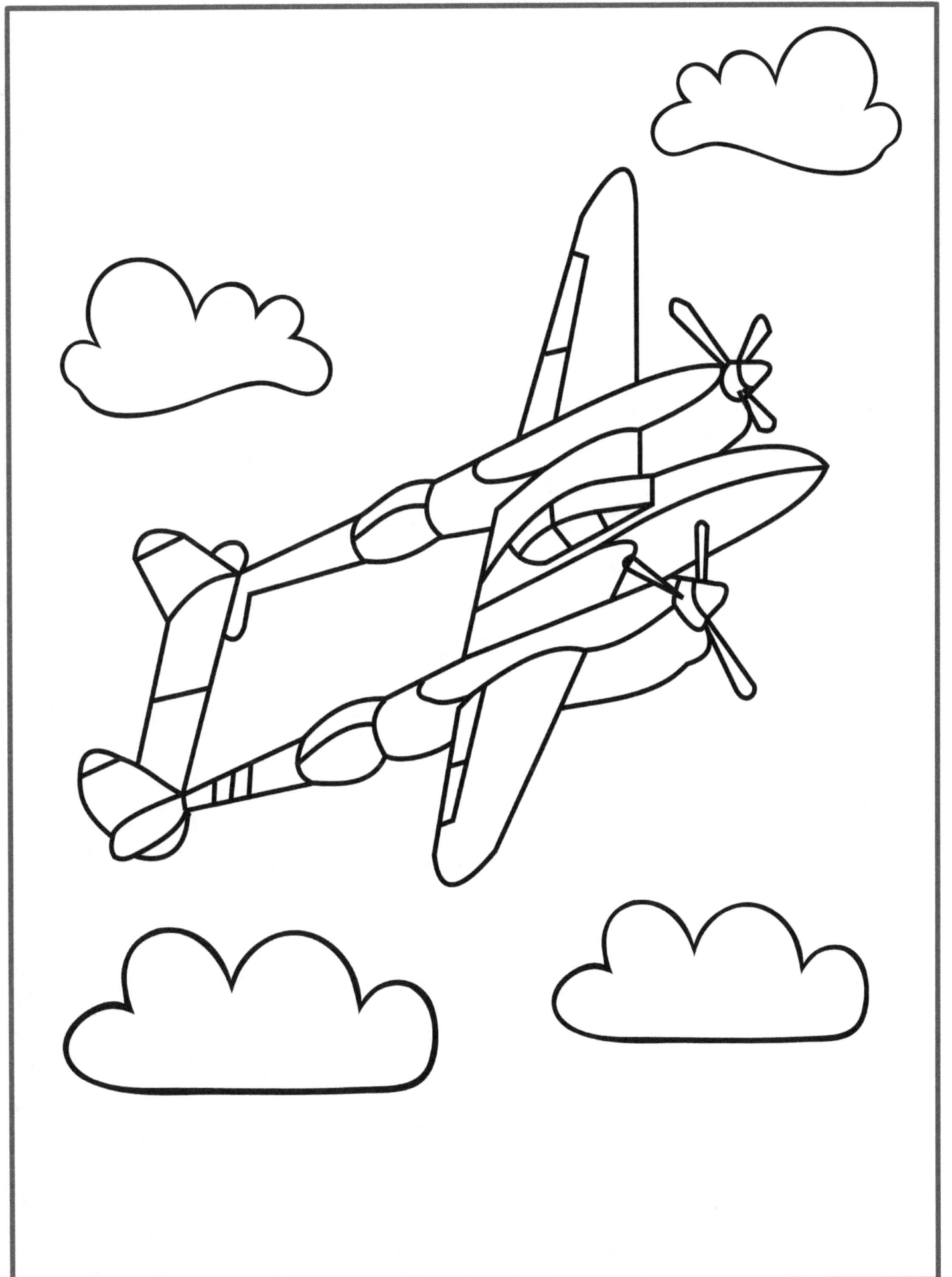

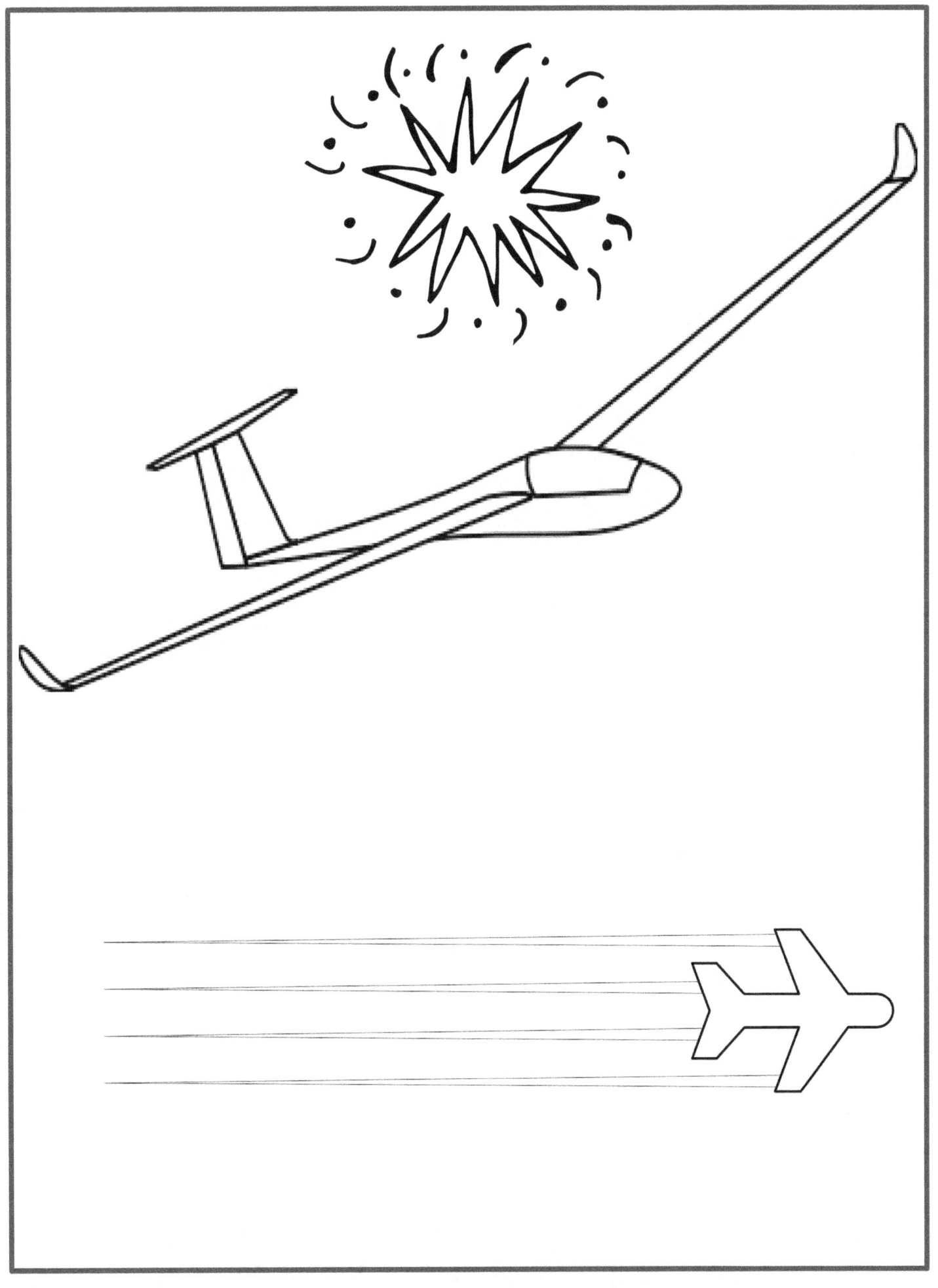

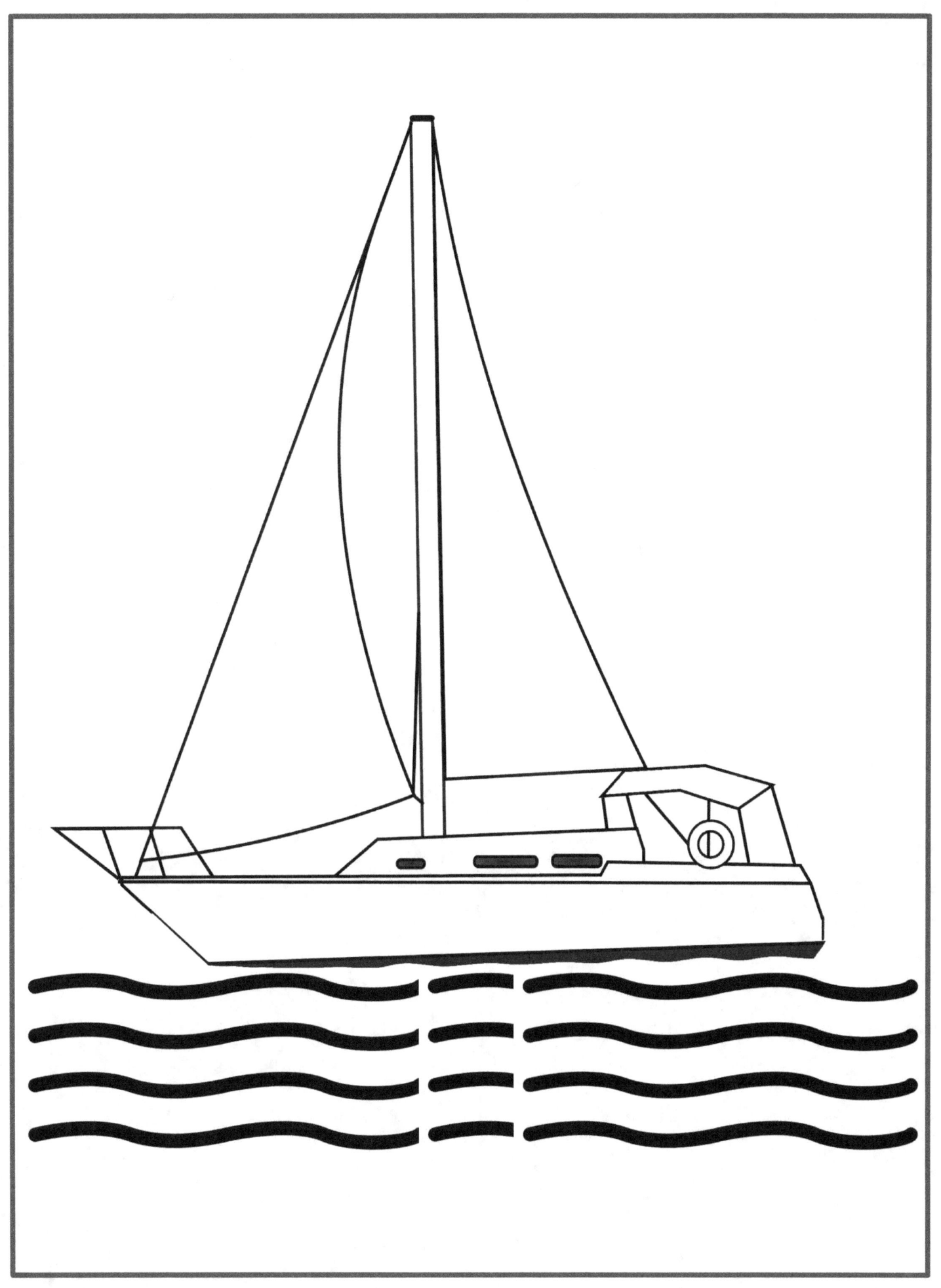

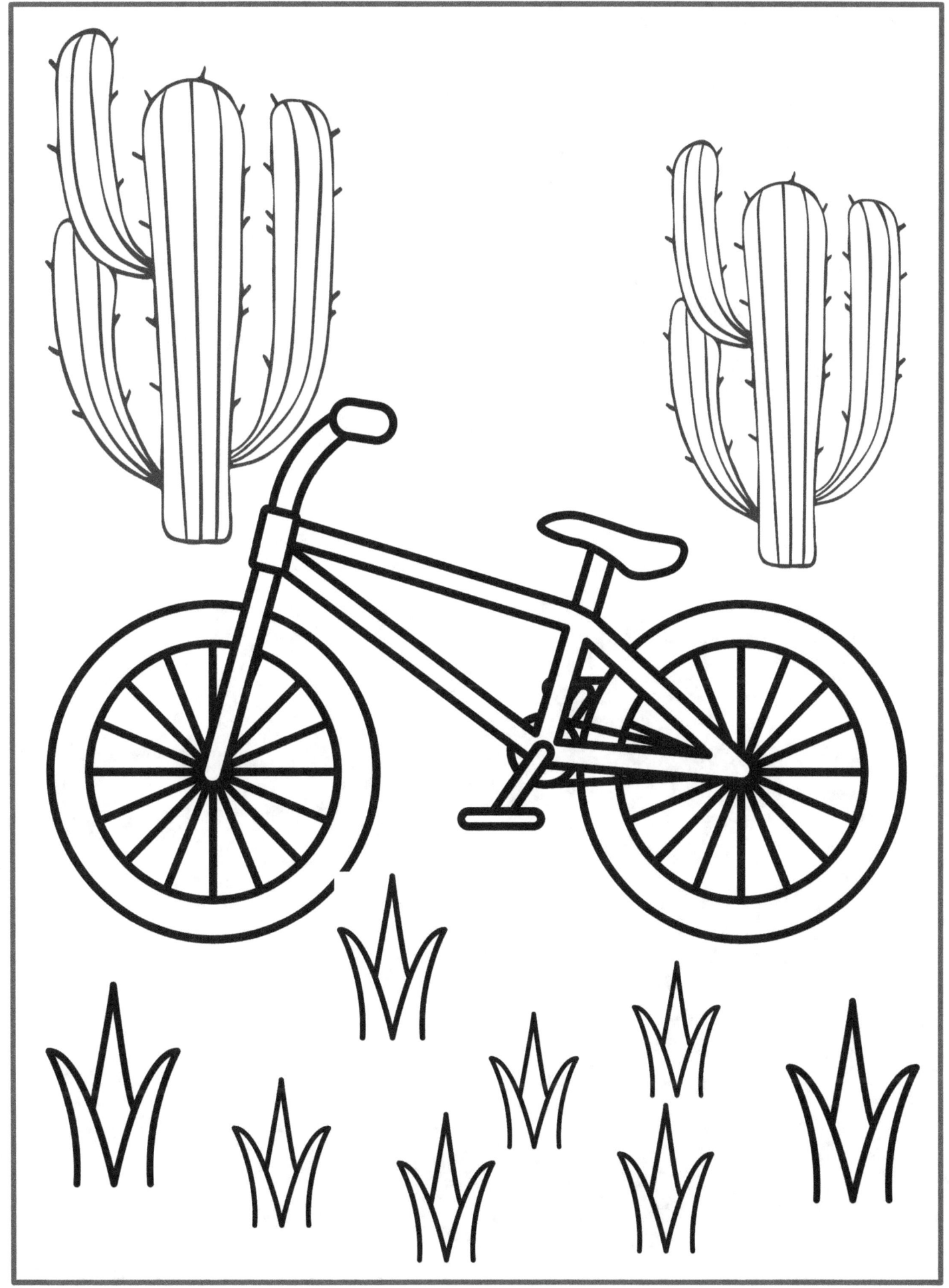

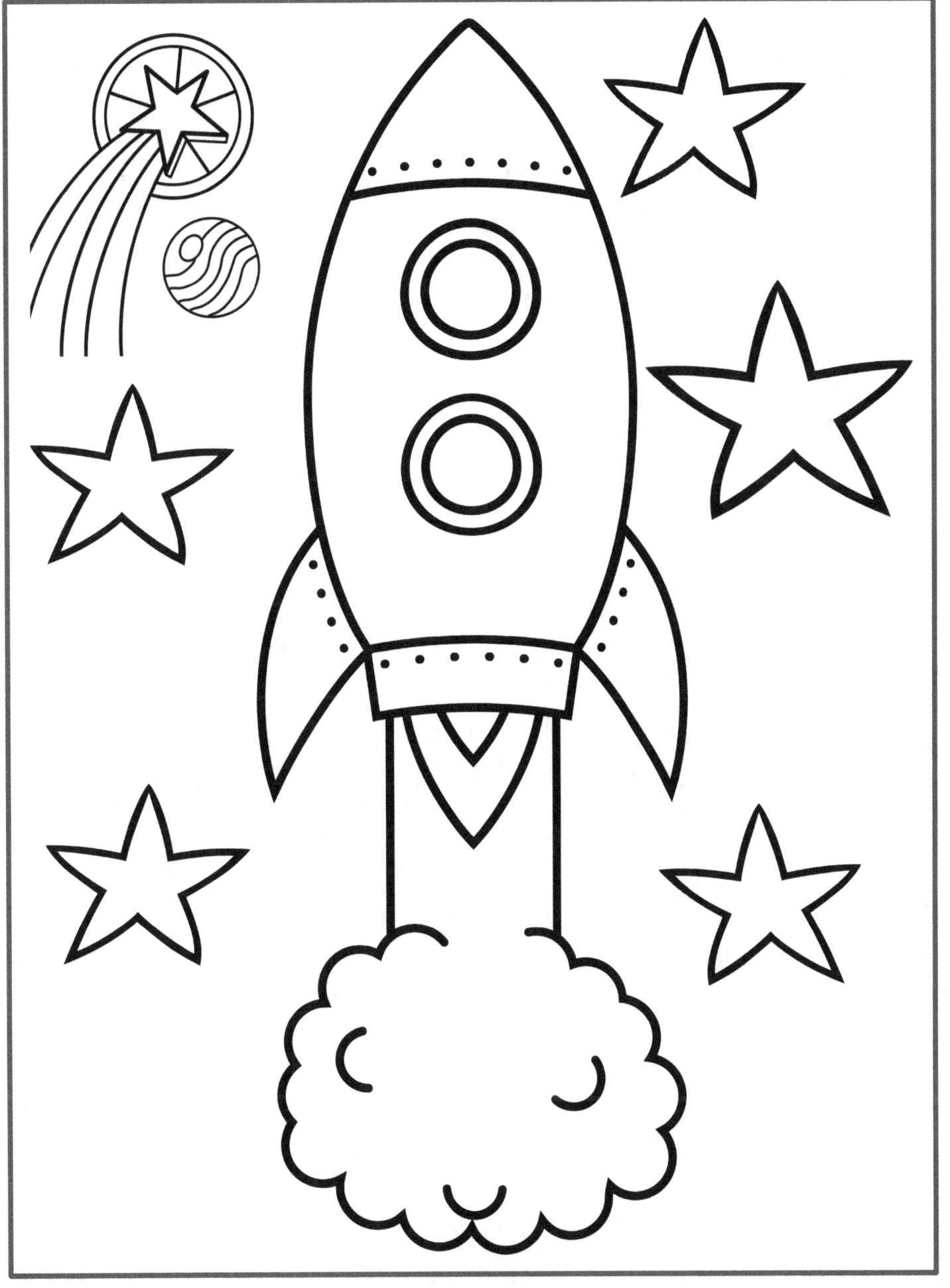

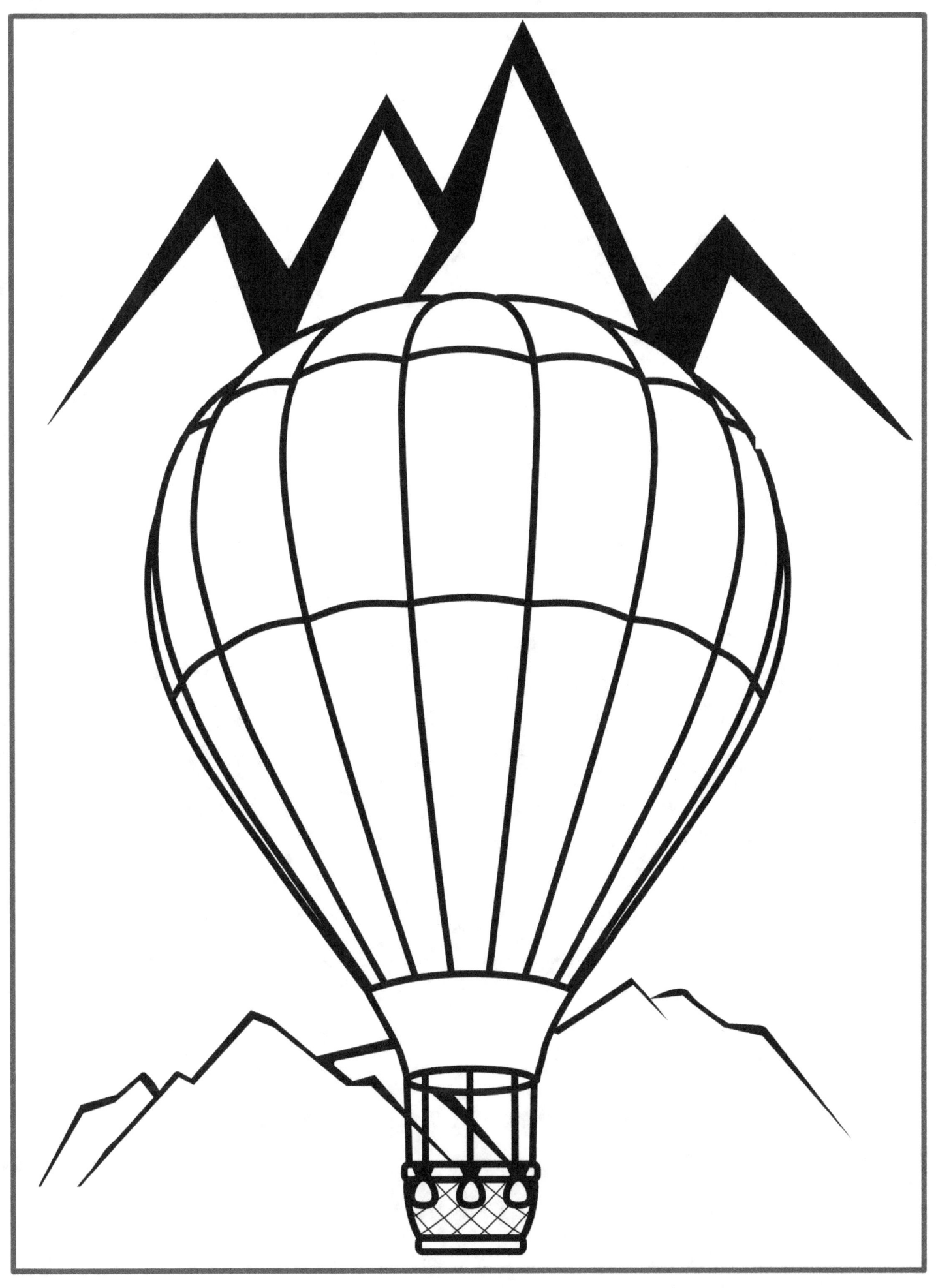

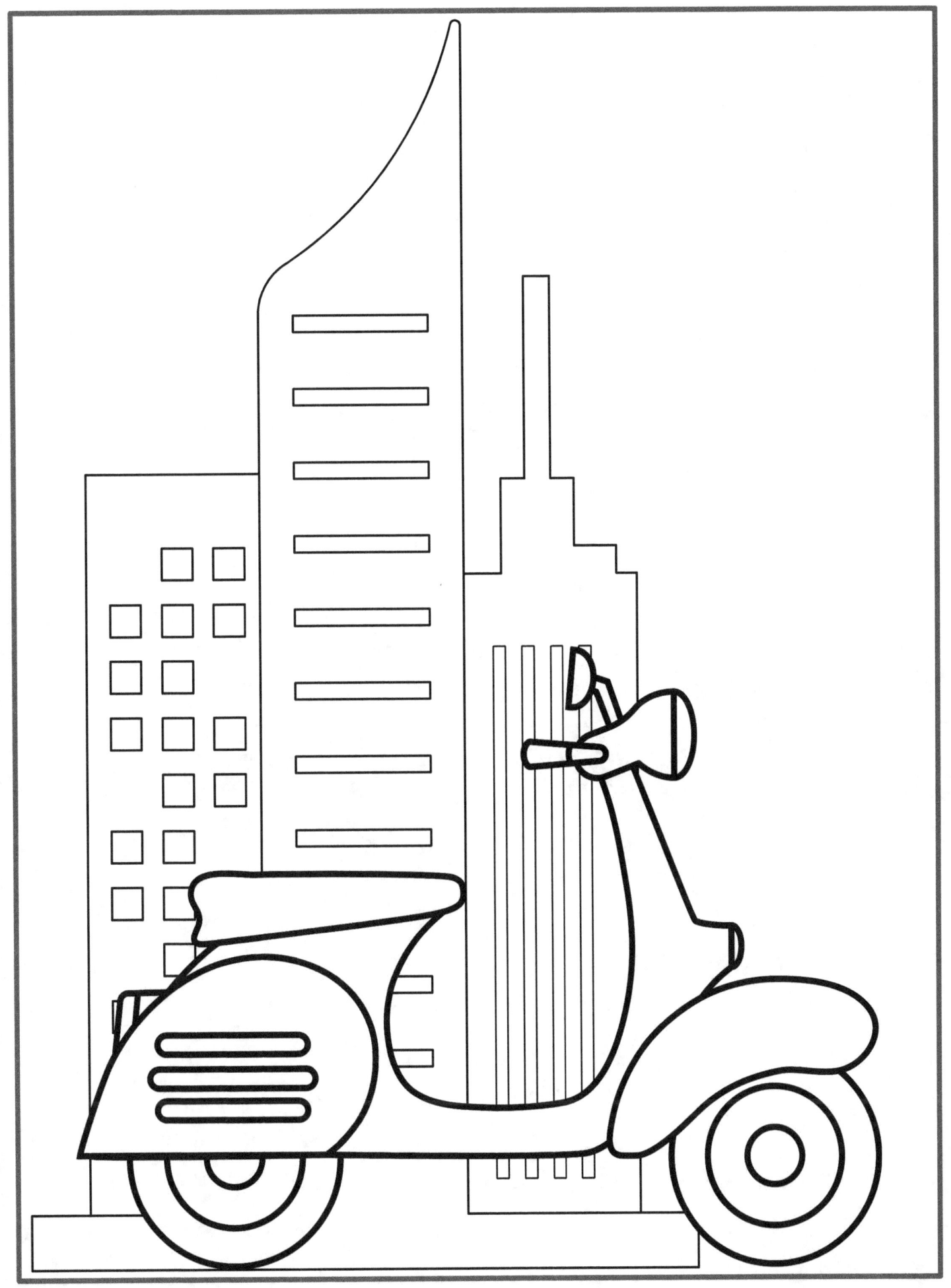

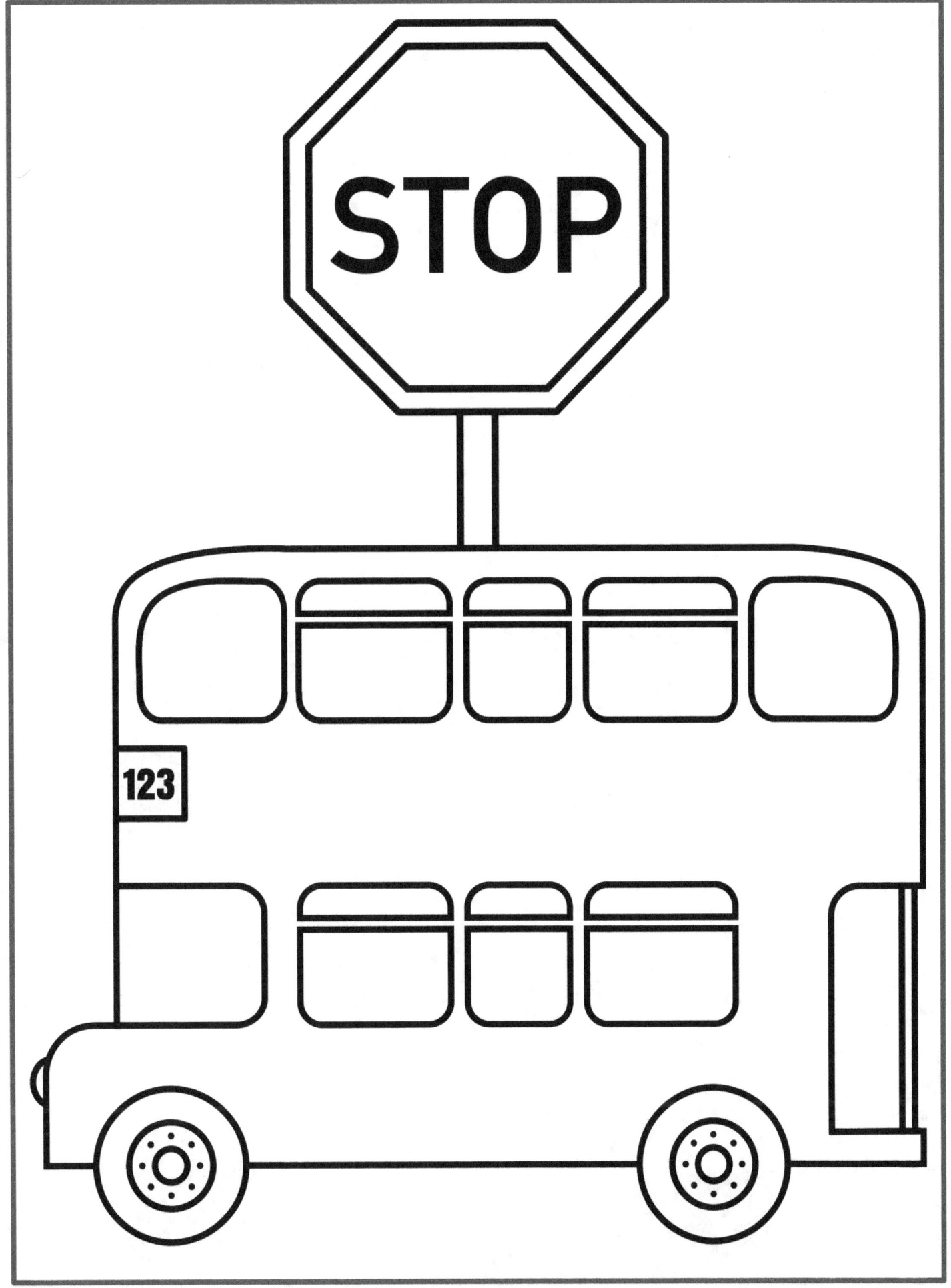

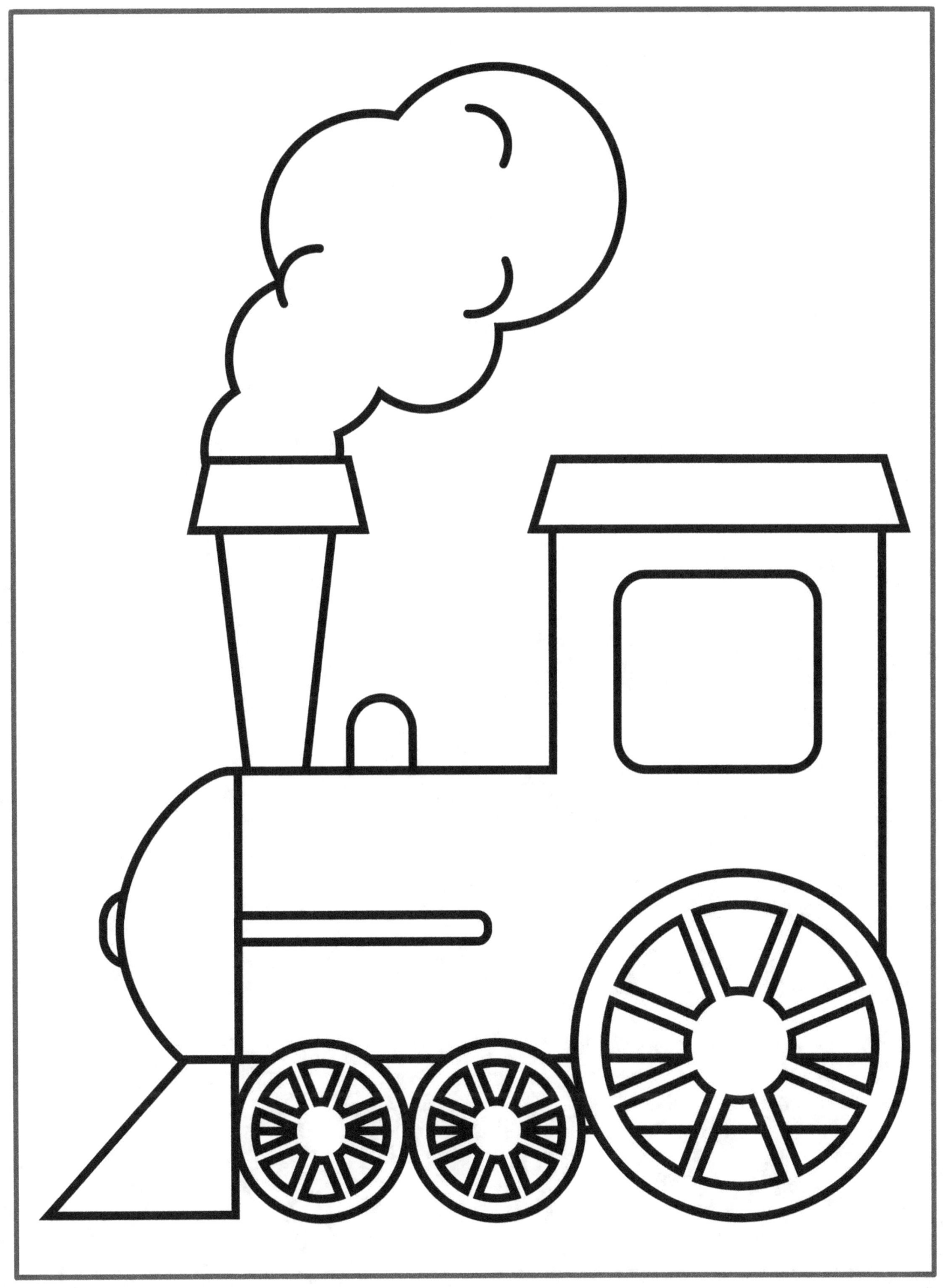

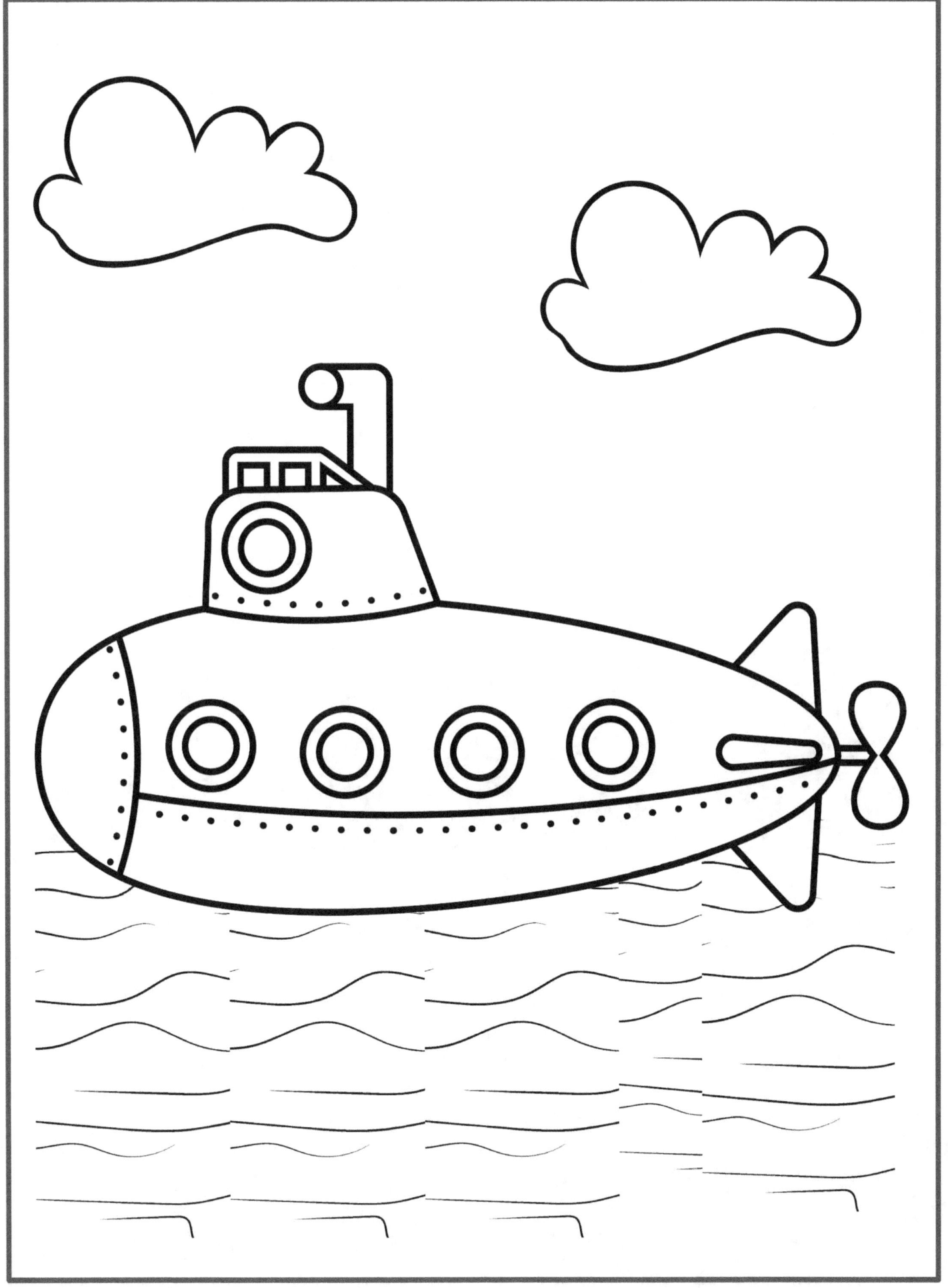

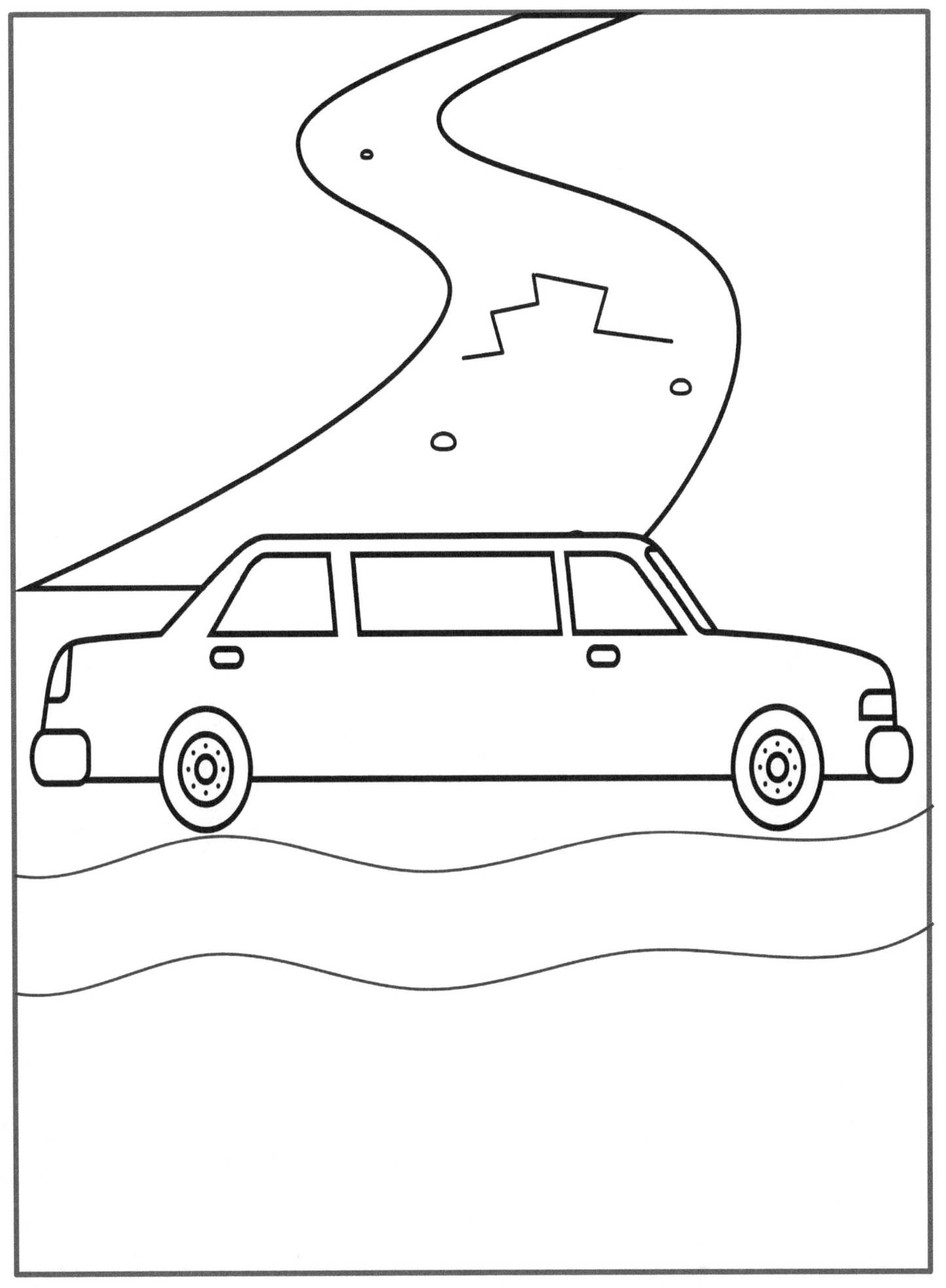

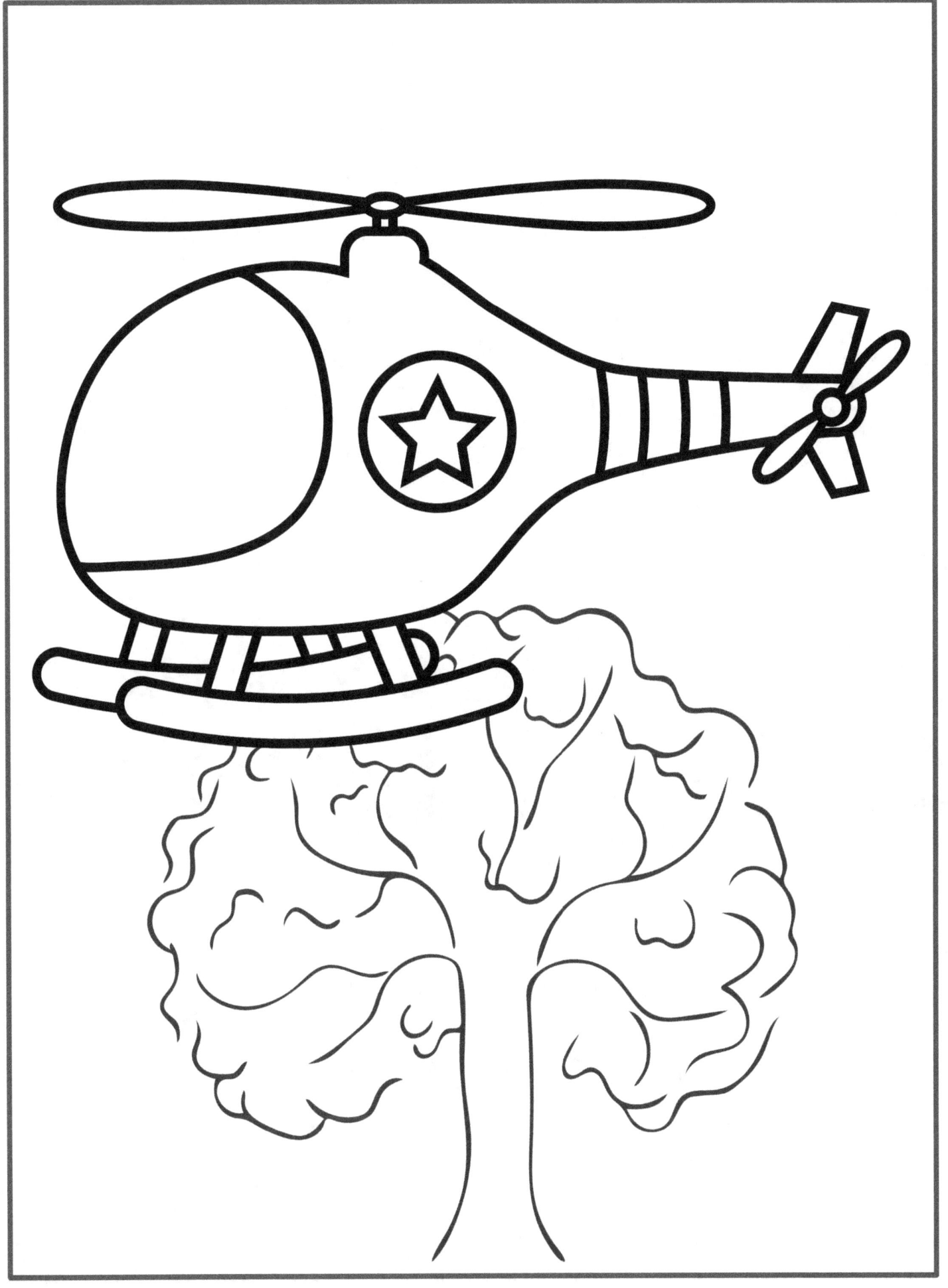

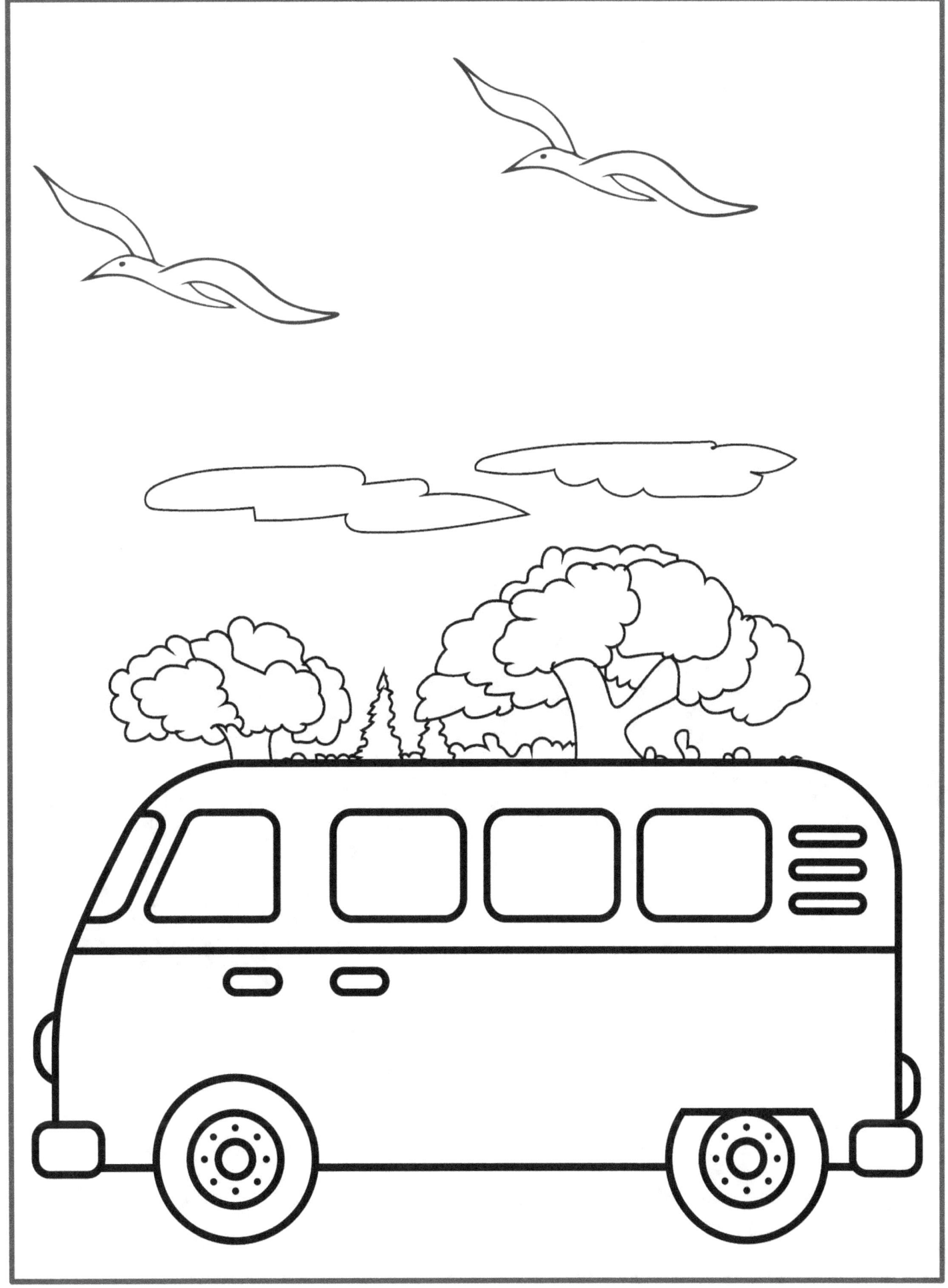

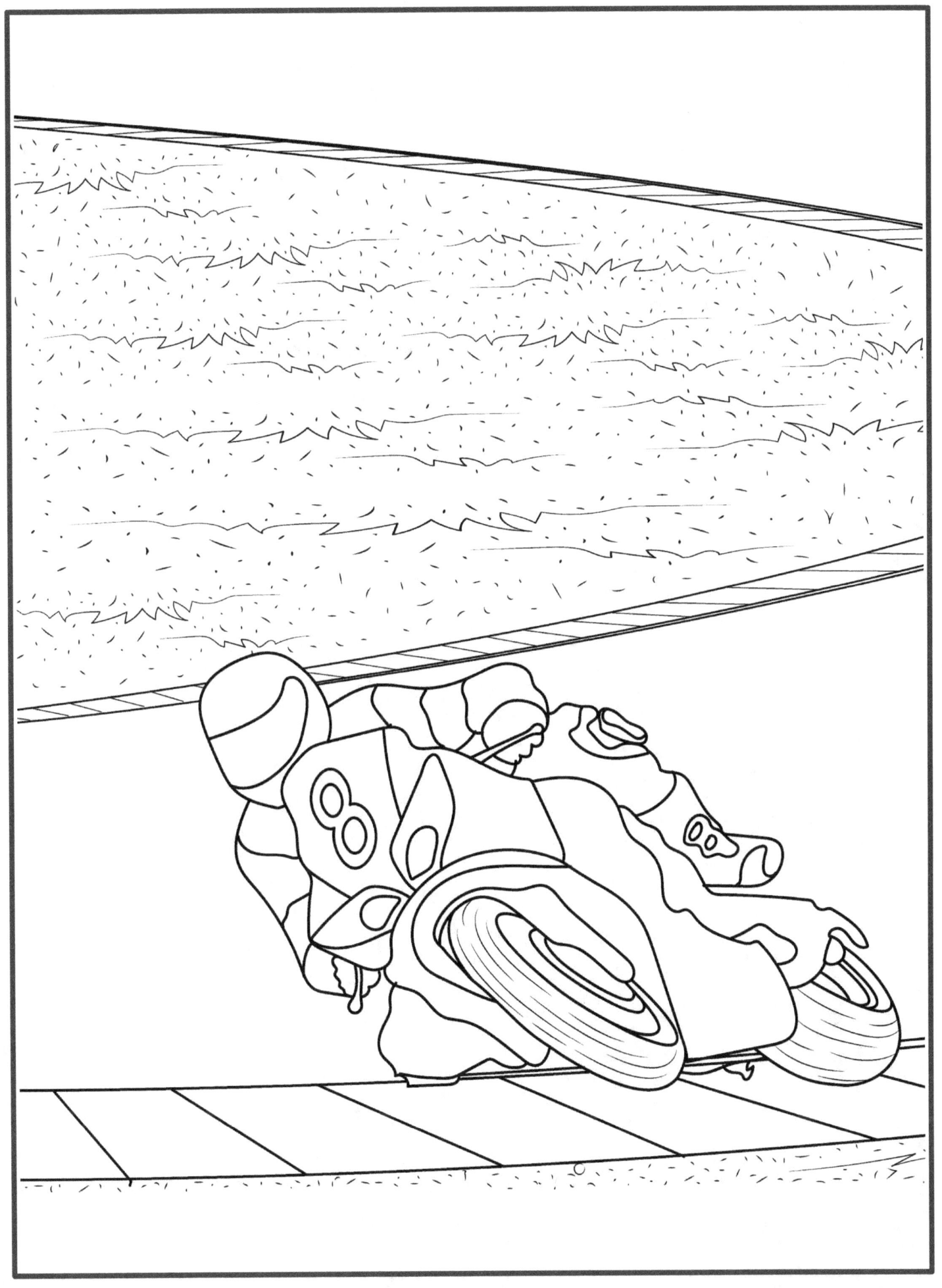

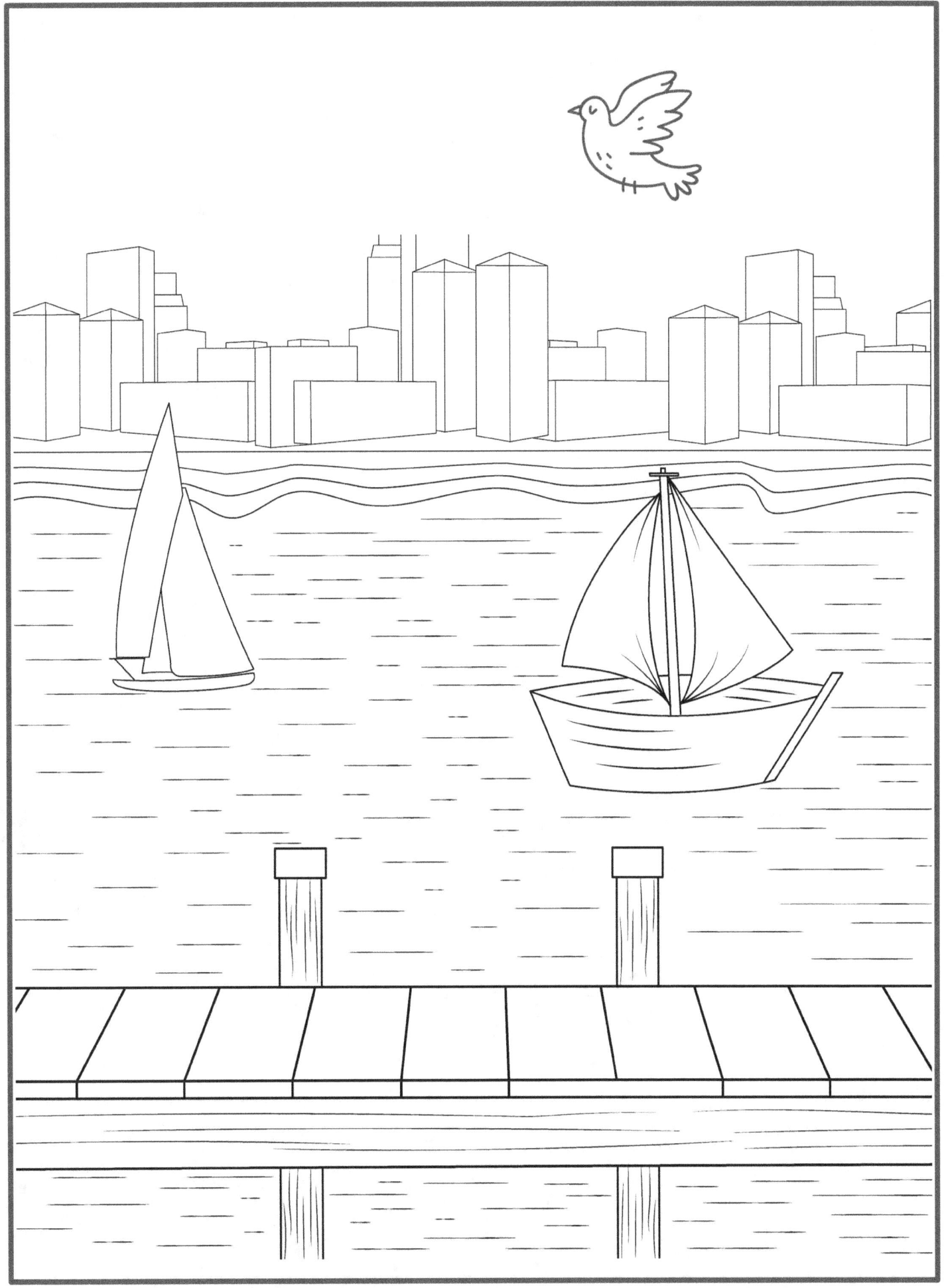

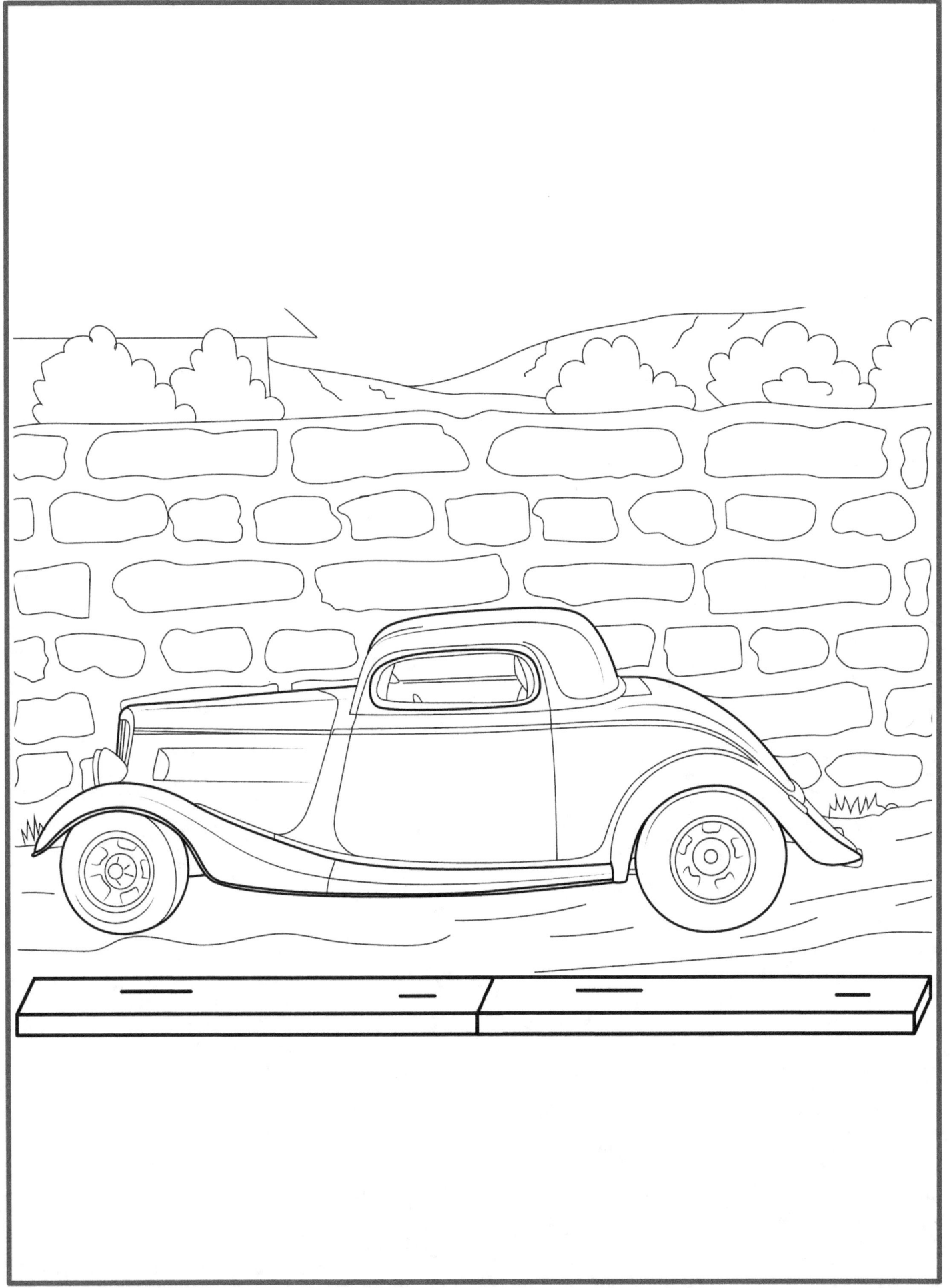

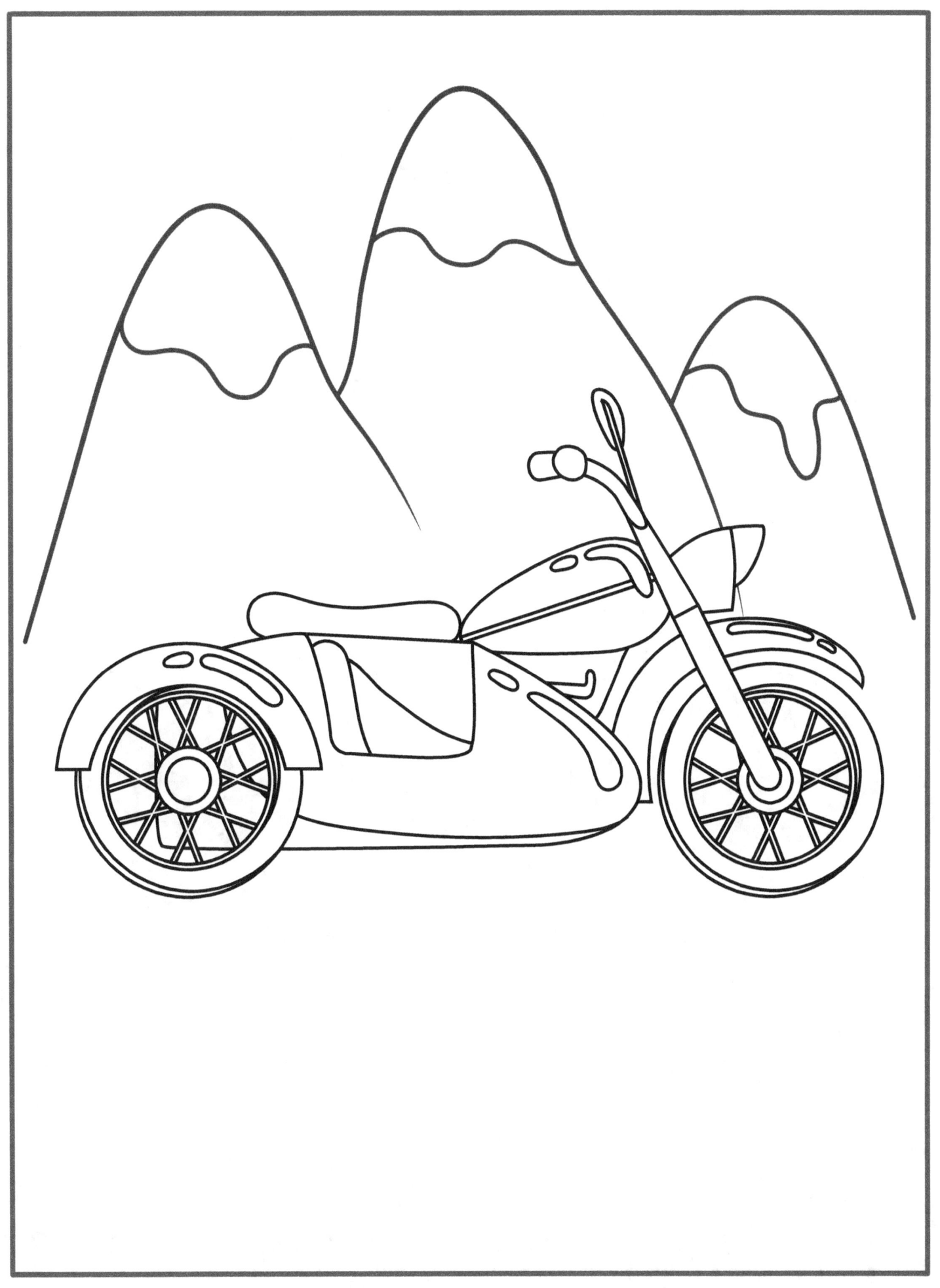

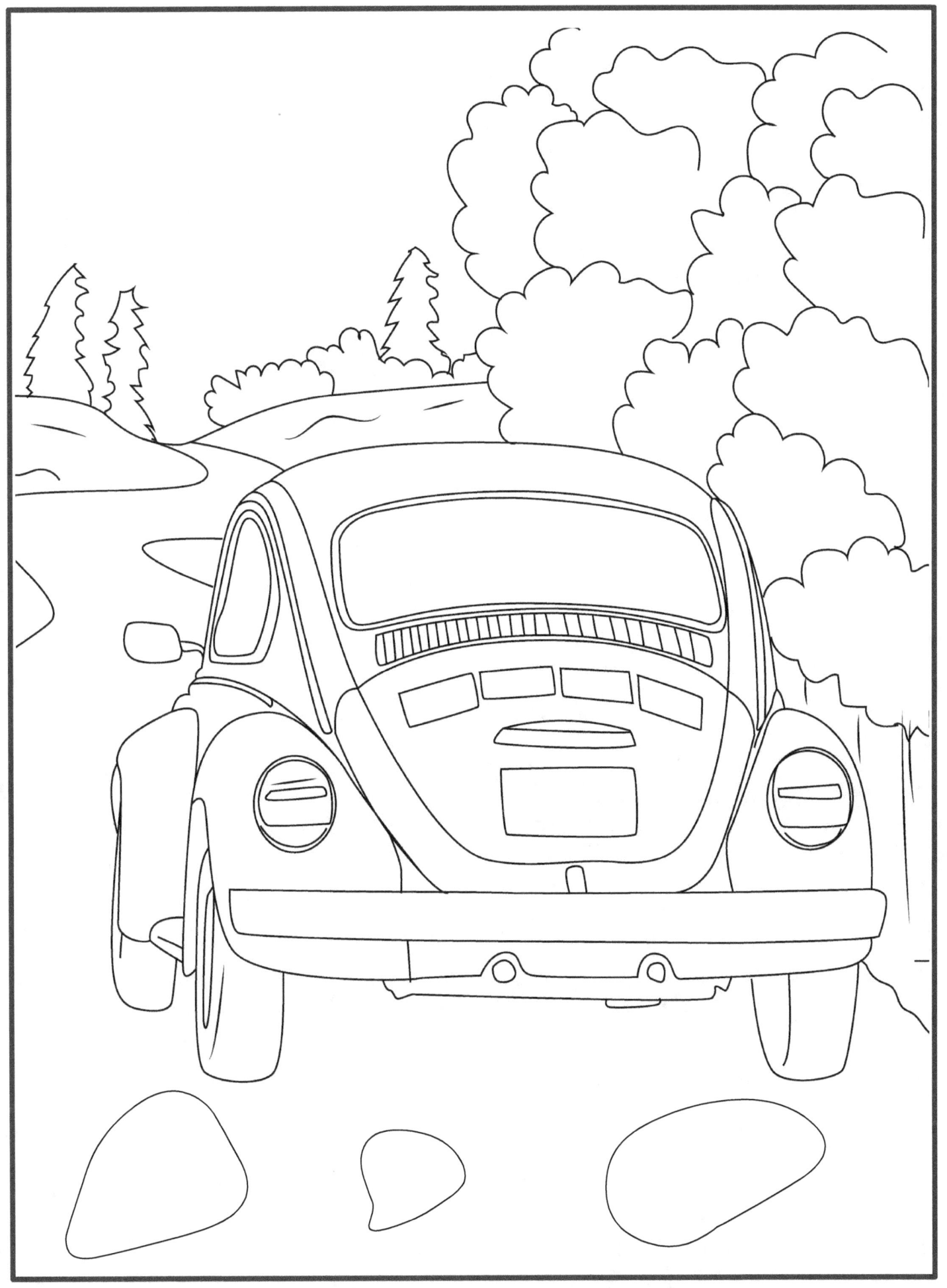

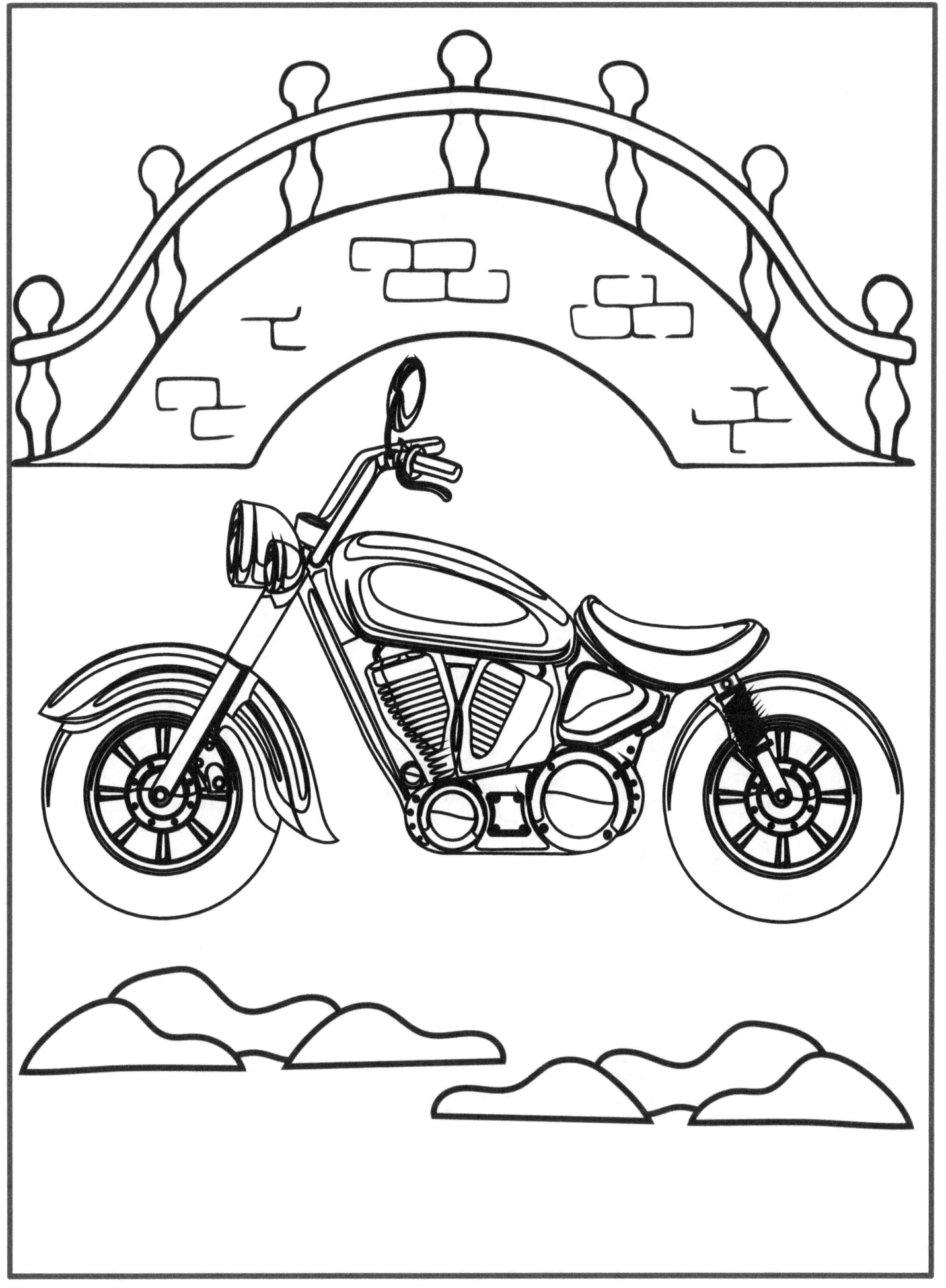

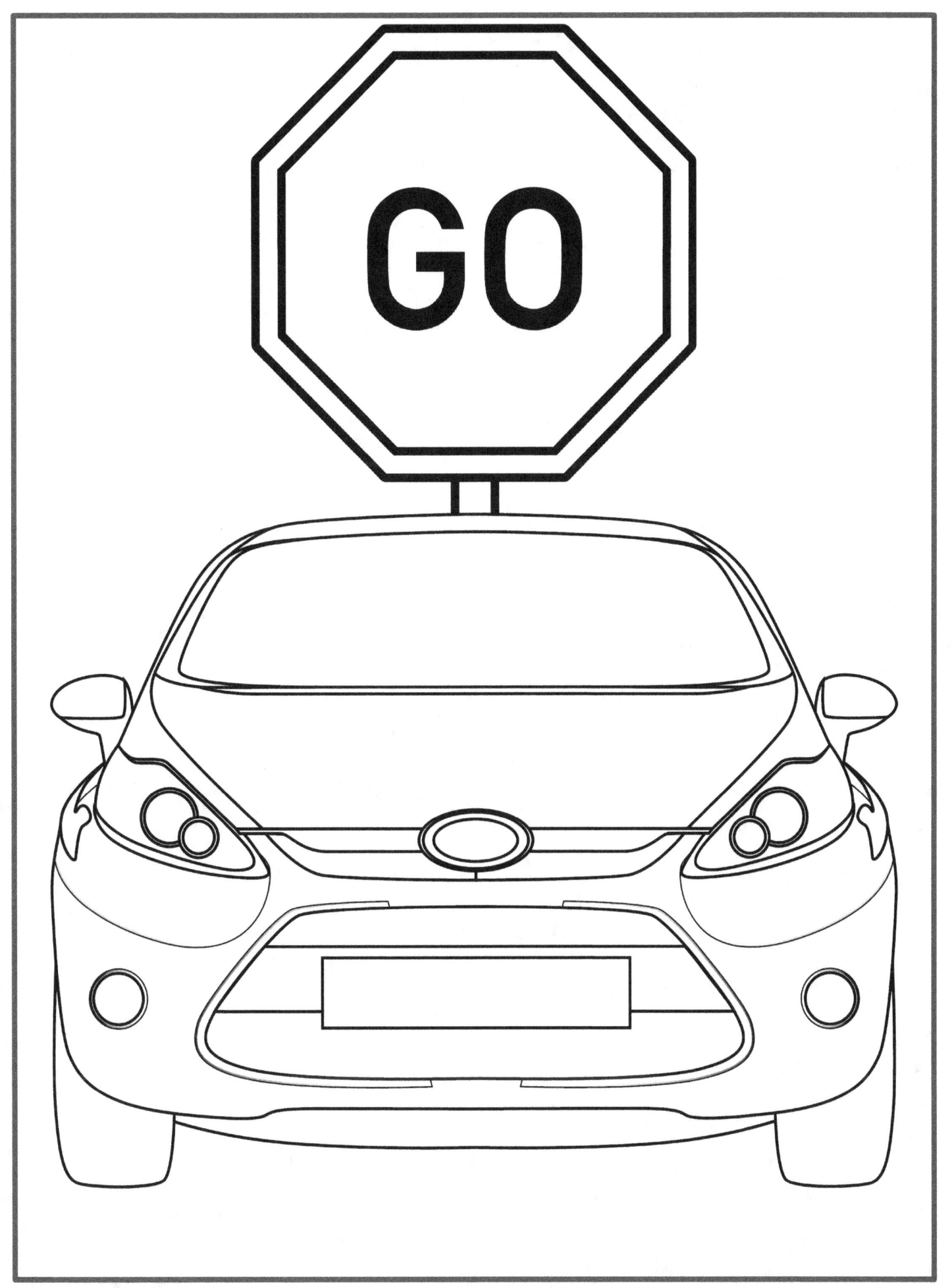

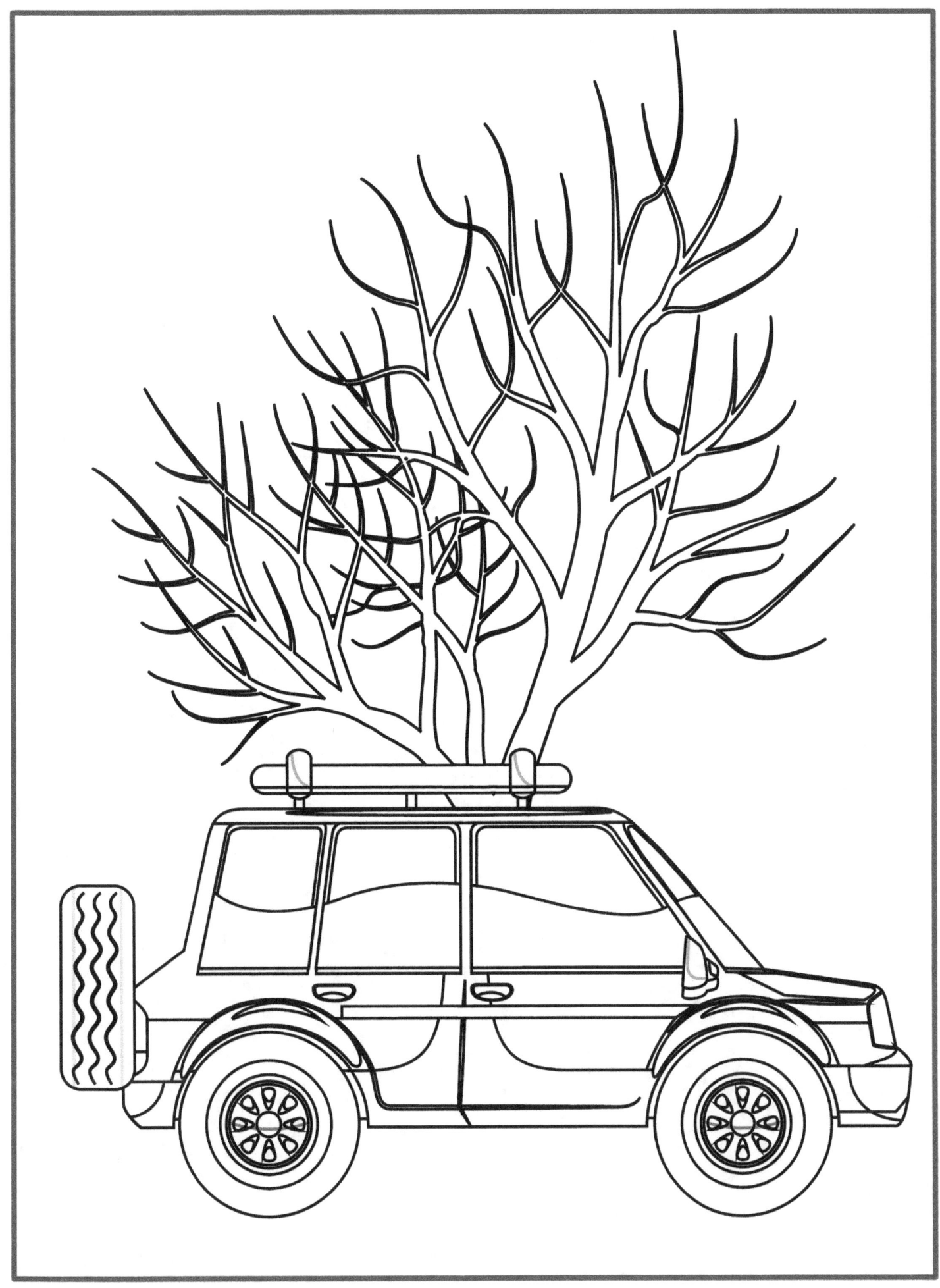

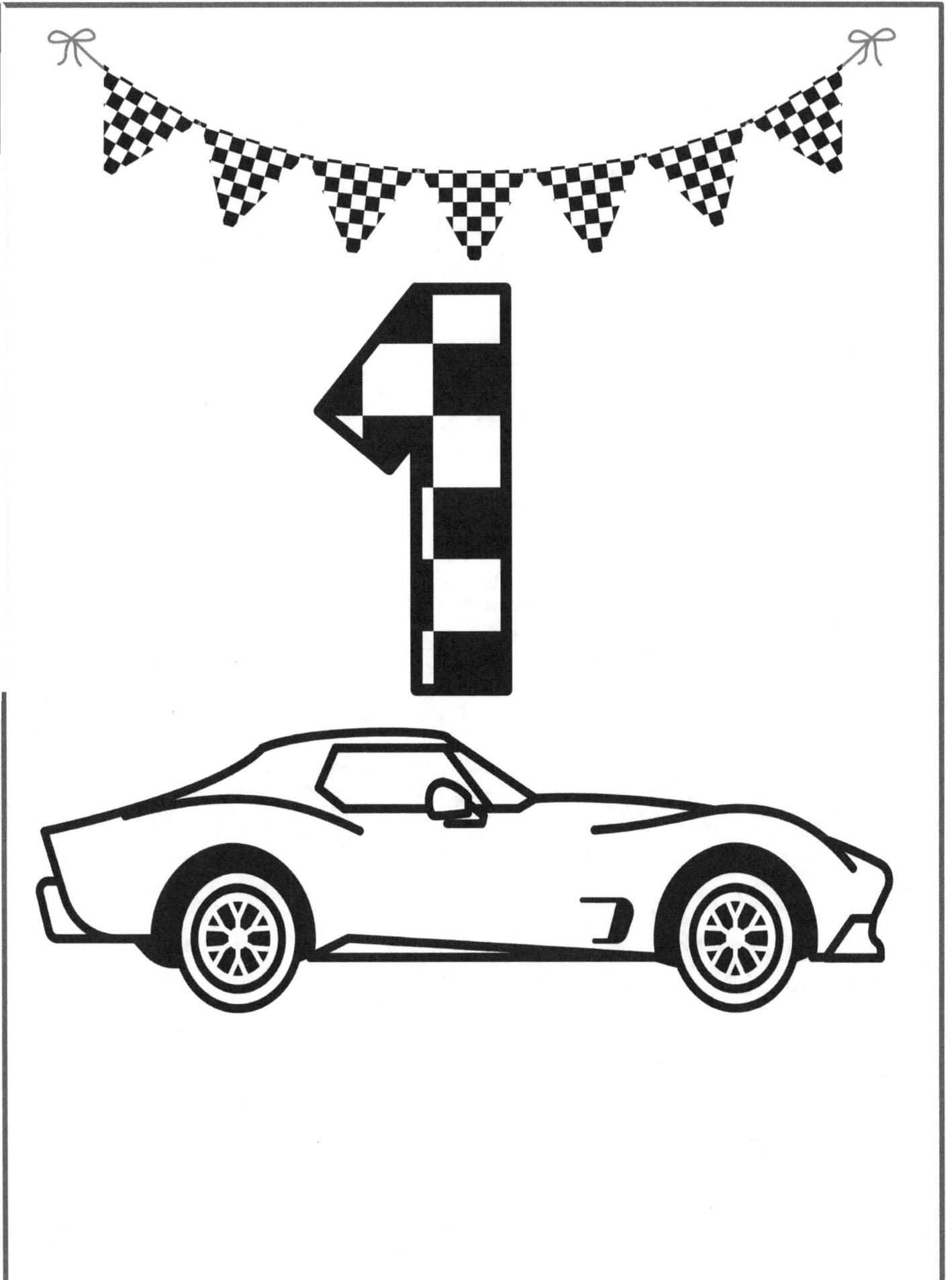

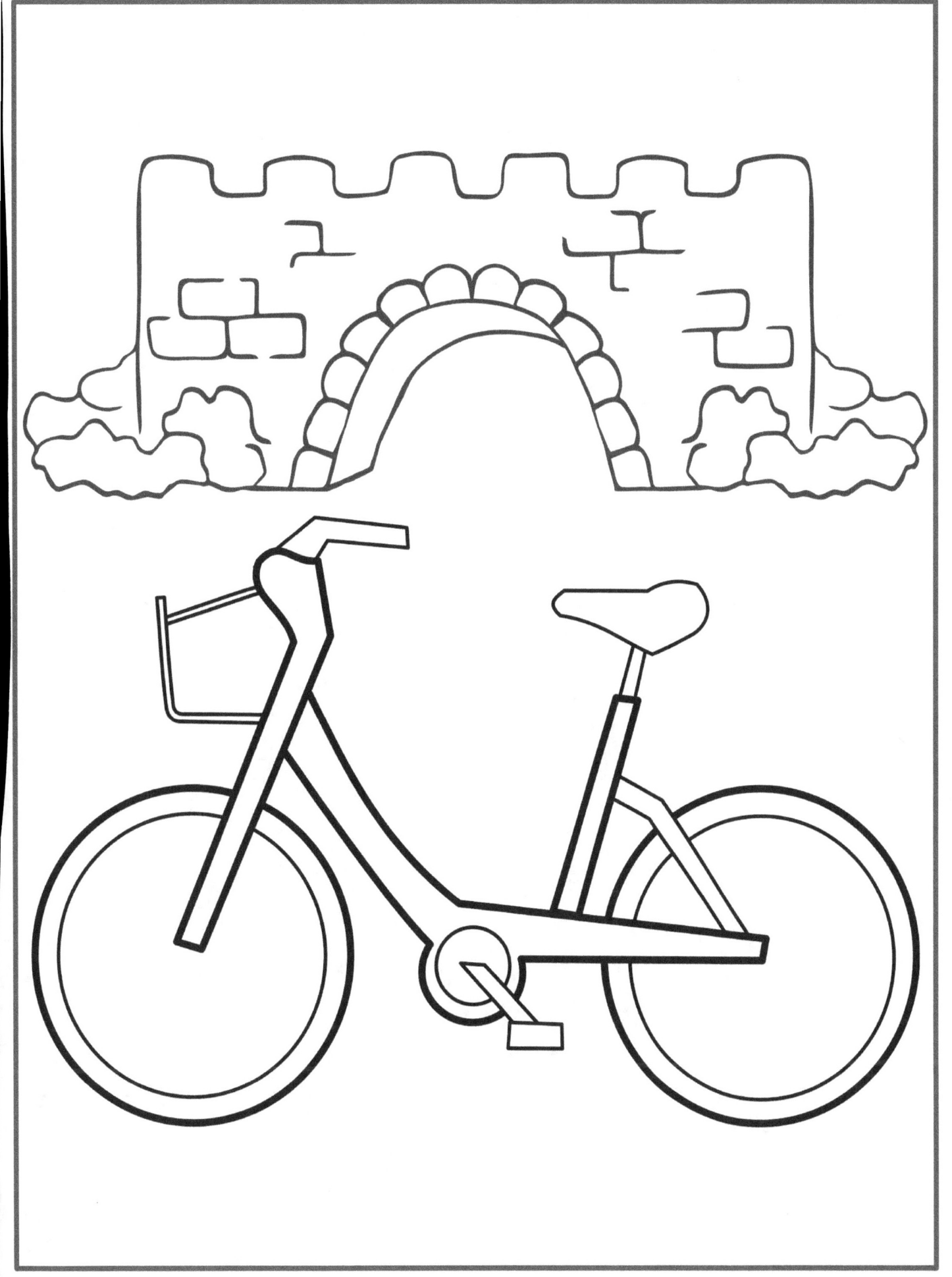

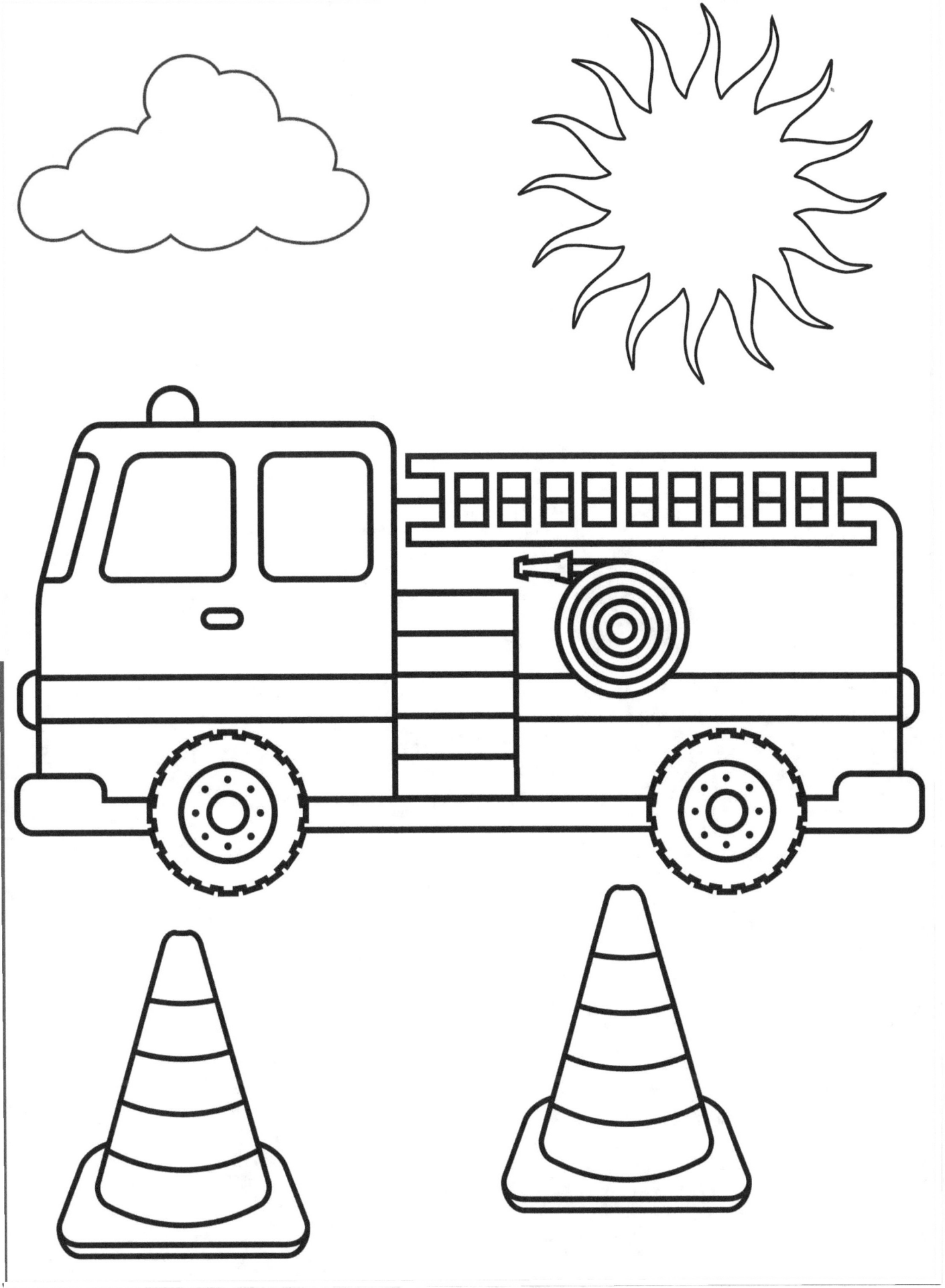

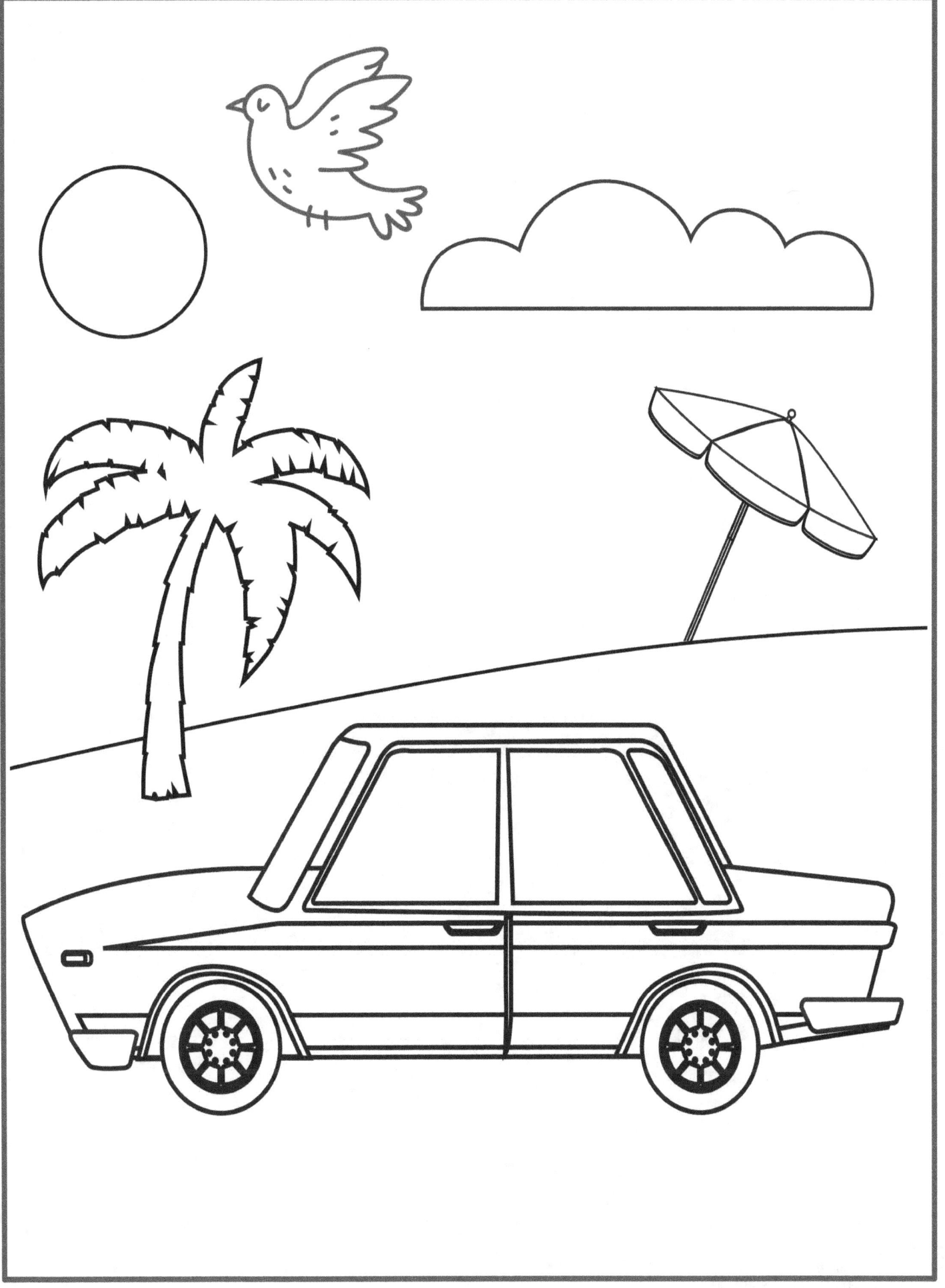

www.ingramcontent.com/pod-product-compliance
Lightning Source LLC
Chambersburg PA
CBHW080514220526
45465CB00006B/2480